my favourite recipes

belongs to

_____

Reader's Digest

Contents

Cooking basics

Remembering a few simple rules can make all the difference to how your cooking efforts transpire. Brush up on your kitchen know-how by perusing the principles below and you'll enjoy perfect results every time.

How to read a recipe

No matter where in the world they originate, modern recipes are generally written in a fairly standard way. The following will help you understand their 'shorthand' tips:

Weights and measurements

❧ Generally, all cup and spoon measurements are level unless stated otherwise.

❧ If a recipe gives both metric and imperial measures, use one or the other; do not mix the two systems.

❧ Can sizes vary between countries and manufacturers; if the specified size is unavailable, use the nearest equivalent.

❧ A small variation in the quantity of most ingredients is unlikely to adversely affect a recipe.

❧ See page 174 for a weights and measures conversion guide.

Ingredients

❧ In most recipes, all fruits and vegetables are medium sized unless stated otherwise.

❧ You should peel any fruits and vegetables (such as apples, bananas, oranges, carrots, garlic, onions, parsnips, potatoes, pumpkin and sweet potatoes) that would normally be peeled before cooking. If they aren't meant to be peeled, the recipe will say so.

❧ All eggs are large unless stated otherwise.

❧ Pasta is dried unless specified otherwise.

❧ Nuts are raw and unsalted unless indicated otherwise.

❧ Dairy foods (such as milk, cream, sour cream and yogurt) are full fat unless the recipe says otherwise. Using a low-fat dairy product in a recipe written for a full-fat product may give a different result.

Oven temperatures

❧ Most recipes are written for regular ovens; if you have a convection (fan-forced) oven, reduce the temperature by 20°C (35°F).

❧ All ovens differ; some run 'hotter' than the temperature indicated on the thermostat. Once you become more accustomed to your oven you will be able to adjust the temperature accordingly.

❧ All ovens have some spots that are hotter than others. This is why recipes will often tell you to put foods on a particular shelf of the oven, or to turn foods around in the oven partway through the cooking time.

Temperature conversions

Celsius (°C)	Fahrenheit (°F)	Gas mark	
–18°C	0°F	–	freezer temperature
0°C	32°F	–	water freezes
82°C	180°F	–	water simmers
100°C	212°F	–	water boils
130°C	265°F	1	low oven
180°C	350°F	4	moderate oven
220°C	425°F	7	hot oven
250°C	475°F	8	very hot oven

Alternative names

Some ingredients are known by different names in different parts of the world. These are a few of the alternative terms for common ingredients:

Buk choy	bok choy
Broad beans	fava beans
Broccolini	tenderstem broccoli
Burghul wheat	bulgur wheat
Capsicum	bell pepper, sweet pepper
Coriander	cilantro
Cornflour	cornstarch
Cos lettuce	romaine lettuce
Cucumber, Lebanese	Mediterranean cucumber
Cucumber, telegraph	long cucumber
Eggplant	aubergine, brinjal
Flat-leaf parsley	Italian parsley, continental parsley
Hazelnut	filbert
Icing	frosting
Icing sugar	confectioner's sugar
Kumara	orange sweet potato
Oregano	origanum
Papaya	pawpaw
Passionfruit	granadilla
Peanuts	ground nuts
Pinto beans	frijoles
Polenta	cornmeal
Prawns	shrimp
Pumpkin	winter squash
Rocket	arugula
Rockmelon	canteloupe, spanspek
Roma tomato	plum tomato
Silverbeet	Swiss chard
Snow peas	mangetout
Spanish onions	red onions
Spring onions	scallions, green onions
Squash, baby	pattypan squash
Sugar, raw	demerara sugar
Sugar, white	granulated sugar
Swede	rutabaga
Tofu	bean curd
Tomato passata	puréed tomatoes, tomato purée
Tomato paste	concentrated purée
Wholemeal	whole-wheat
Witlof	Belgian endive, witloof
Zucchini	courgette, baby marrow

Cooking terms

Acidulate To put foods (such as cut apples) in water mixed with a small amount of lemon juice or vinegar to prevent browning.

Bake blind To bake an empty pastry case with the base weighted down with baking (parchment) paper and dried beans or rice to stop the pastry case rising.

Bruise To slightly crush an ingredient (e.g. a whole garlic clove).

Cube To cut into fairly neat bite-sized chunks.

Deglaze To dissolve the brown sediment left on the bottom of a pan after roasting or frying by adding liquid and stirring.

Dice To first cut into strips then to cut across the strips to make small squares. Large dice are about 2.5 cm (1 inch), medium dice about 1 cm (½ inch) and fine dice about 5 mm (¼ inch).

Dredge/dust To coat lightly; e.g. meat may be dusted with flour before pan-frying, or a cake or dessert may be dusted with icing (confectioners') sugar before serving.

Fold To gently incorporate a light, airy mixture, such as beaten egg whites or whipped cream, into a heavier mixture.

Glaze To brush or coat cooked food (such as a cake or tart) with jam or sugar syrup to give it a glossy finish.

Julienne To cut an ingredient (e.g. carrots) into very fine strips, sometimes called matchsticks.

Knock down/knock back To punch or knead risen dough to push out bubbles that may have formed unevenly shaped holes.

Macerate To soak food, usually fruit, in a syrup or liquid such as alcohol, to allow the flavours to mix.

Purée To reduce to a smooth consistency in a blender, food processor or food mill.

Reduce/reduction To thicken and concentrate the flavour of gravy, sauces, soups and stocks by boiling the liquid down.

Rub in To use the fingertips to combine fat with flour and other dry ingredients until the mixture looks like fine breadcrumbs.

Sauté To fry gently over a low to medium heat.

Scald To heat milk just to the point of boiling.

Sear/seal To brown meat rapidly all over in hot fat.

Shred To finely slice into thin strips; for example, to prepare leafy vegetables for stir-frying.

Sweat To gently fry food, usually vegetables, in butter, oil or a little stock until very soft but not coloured.

Equipping your kitchen

You don't need masses of kitchen equipment to help you cook. Gadgets are all very well, but if you rarely use them they will simply waste space. Here's a list of essential equipment for a smooth-running kitchen. Buy the best you can afford; good-quality equipment will last longer and, in many cases, be easier and more pleasurable to use.

In your cupboards

- Non-stick, heavy-based frying pan with a lid. Choose one with a heatproof handle so it can be transferred to the oven.
- Non-stick wok with a lid, or a deep frying pan.
- Three heavy-based saucepans (small, medium and very large) with lids. Buy the best pans you can afford. Stainless-steel pans with an aluminium base for effective heat transfer will last for many years.
- Cast-iron ridged grill pan.
- Cast-iron flameproof casserole dish. This invaluable item can be used on the stovetop, in the oven and for serving at the table. Although a little pricey, it will last a lifetime.
- Collapsible metal steamer, a steaming pan or steamer inserts that can be tiered on top of your pans.
- Wire cooling rack.
- Metal sieve and free-standing colander.
- Graters (a stainless-steel box grater plus a rotary hand-held grater for grating cheese, nuts and nutmeg).
- Set of mixing bowls – stylish mixing bowls can also double as salad and serving bowls.
- Salad spinner.
- Measuring jug or measuring cup.
- Citrus squeezer or juicer.
- Electric mixer, for whipping cream, egg whites, sauces and batters and for making creamy mashed potatoes.
- Ovenproof gratin dish for bakes.
- Set of weighing scales. Electronic digital scales are accurate and can switch from metric to imperial and back to zero instantly at the press of a button. An 'add and weigh' feature allows you to measure out an entire recipe in one bowl.
- Hand-held stick blender. This can be used as a mini food processor to quickly purée soups and sauces in the pan, rather than having to transfer the food to a worktop processor or blender. A wall-mounted version is handy for immediate use.

On your benchtop

- Salt and pepper mills.
- Knife block with a selection of good sharp knives, including a long serrated bread knife, a medium-sized cook's knife (about an 18 cm/7 inch blade), essential for chopping

and slicing meat and vegetables, and a small cook's knife or curved paring knife (about a 7.5 cm/3 inch blade), for smaller jobs like paring or peeling. A top-quality knife makes food preparation easier, faster and safer – accidents happen when trying to hack through food using a semi-blunt knife. A knife with a stainless-steel blade and a steel-lined handle is best. These knives are dishwasher-proof and do not rust. A good knife will last for many years.

- Chopping boards – keep different ones for raw and cooked food, and possibly a small one for flavourings. Plastic boards can often be bought in sets of three: red for raw meat, green for vegetables and white for cooked foods.
- A roll of paper towels.

In the top drawer

- Vegetable peeler.
- Garlic crusher.
- Can opener.
- Pair of sharp kitchen scissors.
- Set of measuring spoons.
- Corkscrew.
- Metal skewers.
- Rolling pin.
- Knife sharpener or sharpening steel.
- Pizza wheel.

In a large utensil pot (next to the stove)

- Selection of wooden or heatproof plastic spoons.
- Large metal spoon and ladle.
- Large slotted spoon.
- Potato masher.
- Long-handled, non-stick, wide metal spatula.
- Non-stick plastic spatulas.
- Pair of tongs.

In the oven drawer or a kitchen cupboard

- Roasting tin (baking pan).
- Baking sheet. Buy a non-stick one made from heavy-gauge aluminium or steel, which won't warp or buckle.
- Baking tray (with a raised edge) for foods that may spill.
- Muffin pan and cake tins.

Optional extras

- Pressure cooker. Cooking food in a pressurised container reduces cooking time dramatically and is particularly valuable for tougher cuts of meat and for poultry, soups, stocks, root vegetables and dried pulses.

Food processor. This machine will take many laborious food preparation chores off your hands. It will chop, mince, mix, purée, shred and grate, whiz up cake mixtures and make pastry and dough, giving perfect results in seconds. Use it for grating cheese, chopping nuts, making breadcrumbs, mixing smooth creamy sauces, dressings and dips and puréeing or blending soups. Find a space for your food processor on the benchtop where it's always close to hand.

Blender. Ideal for liquidising soups and sauces and for making smoothies and fruit purées. Can also be used on the pulse setting to make breadcrumbs or to grind nuts. If you also have a hand-held blender and/or a food processor, you might find that a blender becomes redundant.

Electric grinder. As well as grinding coffee beans, this can be used to grind nuts and make breadcrumbs – especially useful if you often prepare vegetarian dishes. This gadget is also good for grinding spices, although it's best to have one for coffee and one for spices, to avoid the flavours mixing.

Specialist equipment such as pasta machines, bread-makers and ice-cream machines are great if you enjoy making such foods, and the results are rewarding, but otherwise they are unlikely to be used often.

Alternative names

Sometimes kitchen utensils and equipment are known by different names. Here are a few of the alternative terms for some common items:

baking paper	parchment paper
fish slice/egg flip	spatula
flan tin	tart pan
grill	broiler
loaf tin	bar tin, loaf pan
roasting tin	baking pan, baking dish, roasting pan
tea towel	dish towel

Soups

Nourishing, easy to make and incredibly versatile,
soup makes a comforting starter or the ultimate one-pot meal.
All the ingredients are simmered together in a nutritious
stock, retaining all of their goodness.

Basics

*Although you can buy ready-made stocks, it's usually cheaper,
healthier and tastier to make your own. They take very little preparation
or effort — just an hour or two of gentle, lazy simmering.
Why not make a double batch and freeze the rest for later use?*

Chicken stock

Place 1 chicken carcass or the remains of a roasted chicken in
a large saucepan or stockpot with 10 cups (2.5 litres/88 fl oz)
cold water. Bring to a boil, skimming off any froth that rises
to the surface, then add 1 chopped onion, 1 chopped carrot,
1 chopped celery stalk, 1 trimmed and sliced leek, 1 fresh or dried
bouquet garni (made from a bay leaf, some parsley and thyme),
6 whole black peppercorns and ½ teaspoon salt. Partially cover
the pan, reduce the heat and simmer for 2 hours, or until the
liquid has reduced by just over half. Remove the pan from the
heat and strain the stock, discarding the bones and vegetables.
Leave to cool, then skim off any fat. Refrigerate for up to 4 days,
or freeze for up to 6 months. Makes 4 cups (1 litre/35 fl oz).

Beef stock

Preheat the oven to 220°C (425°F/Gas 7). Place 750 g–1 kg
(1½ –2 lb) beef bones in a large baking dish with a little oil and
brown them in the oven for 20 minutes. Put the bones in a large
saucepan or stockpot and pour in 10 cups (2.5 litres/ 88 fl oz)
cold water. Bring to a boil, skimming off any froth that rises
to the surface, then add 1 chopped onion, 1 chopped carrot,
1 chopped celery stalk, 1 fresh or dried bouquet garni, 6 whole
black peppercorns and ½ teaspoon salt. Partially cover the pan,
reduce the heat and simmer for 2 hours, or until the liquid has
reduced by just over half. Remove the pan from the heat and
strain the stock, discarding the bones and vegetables. Leave to
cool, then skim off any fat. Refrigerate for up to 4 days, or freeze
for up to 6 months. Makes 4 cups (1 litre/35 fl oz).

Vegetable stock

Peel, trim and roughly chop 750 g–1 kg (1½ –2 lb) mixed
fresh vegetables, such as beans, cauliflower, celery, leeks,
onions and any type of root vegetable. (For the best flavour,
choose vegetables that are in season; this also ensures a more
nutritious stock.) Place in a large saucepan or stockpot and
pour in 6 cups (1.5 litres/52 fl oz) cold water. Add 1 bouquet
garni, a large strip of lemon zest, 6 whole peppercorns and
1 teaspoon salt. Bring to a boil, then reduce the heat, partially
cover the pan and simmer gently for 45 minutes, or until the
liquid has reduced by one-third. Remove the pan from the heat
and strain the stock, discarding the vegetables. Leave to cool,
then refrigerate for up to 4 days, or freeze for up to 6 months.
Makes 4 cups (1 litre/35 fl oz).

Fish stock

Pour 5 cups (1.25 litres/44 fl oz) cold water into a large
saucepan or stockpot. Add 1 kg (2 lb) trimmings from non-oily
white fish (except the gills and guts), or use 500 g (16 oz) white
fish fillets. Add ½ cup (125 ml/4 fl oz) dry white wine and
1 sliced onion. Bring to a boil and cook gently over low heat for
5 minutes. Skim off any froth that rises to the surface, then add
1 bouquet garni, 1 tablespoon lemon juice and 4 whole black
peppercorns. Partially cover the pan, reduce the heat, then
simmer gently for 20–30 minutes. Remove from the heat and
strain the stock, discarding the solids. Leave to cool, then
refrigerate for up to 4 days, or freeze for up to 6 months.
Makes 4 cups (1 litre/35 fl oz).

Hints and tips

Stocks

🌿 Vegetables should be washed and peeled.

🌿 For best results, use good-quality ingredients for stock, rather than meats and vegetables that are past their best.

🌿 Bones, meats and vegetables can be used raw, or can be roasted first to give a deeper flavour. Using bones will make the stock richer in B vitamins.

🌿 If bones are not available, use inexpensive poultry portions such as wings (skinned) or necks, or inexpensive cuts of meat such as stewing beef or lamb.

🌿 Ham hocks or ham bones make great stock. Such bones are often salty, so it's a good idea to first soak them in cold water for a few hours, then drain and rinse before using. If you're short of time, use them as is, but remember to taste the finished soup before adding extra salt.

🌿 Trim all visible fat from meat and bones.

🌿 When making stock, always start with cold water and bring slowly to a boil. This allows more impurities to rise to the surface, where they can be removed using a skimmer or large metal spoon.

🌿 Once the stock has come to a boil, reduce the heat and allow to simmer gently. This extracts maximum flavour and stops the ingredients disintegrating.

🌿 Skim stocks regularly to ensure a clean, clear stock.

🌿 Be sparing when adding salt; simmering the stock concentrates the flavour, so it may end up too salty.

🌿 Allow the finished stock to cool a little, then strain through a large sieve, preferably lined with muslin (cheesecloth) to catch the smallest particles. Allow the liquid to drip through on its own rather than pressing on the solids, which will make the stock cloudy.

🌿 Let the stock cool to room temperature, then cover and chill for several hours or overnight before skimming off any fat that has solidified on the surface. The stock is now ready to be used or frozen.

Soups

🌿 If a soup contains cream, sour cream or yogurt, add it towards the end of the cooking time and do not allow the soup to boil again.

🌿 If a soup is too thin, simmer it for a little longer to reduce it, or add a starchy ingredient such as potatoes, barley or rice. If it is too thick, thin it with water, stock or milk.

🌿 If a soup is too salty, add a whole potato and simmer for 20–30 minutes. The potato will soak up some of the excess salt. Discard the potato before serving.

🌿 For a smooth-textured soup, let it cool a little, then purée it (in batches if necessary) in a blender or food processor. If you want to retain a little texture, either purée it roughly, or keep part of the mixture unpuréed and stir it back into the soup. For a coarser texture, mash the mixture in the pan with a potato masher.

Storing and freezing stocks and soups

🌿 Homemade stocks and soups are great for using up a glut of seasonal produce. Make up several batches and freeze in useful quantities or serving portions for up to 6 months.

🌿 To freeze stock or soup, pour it into a container lined with a polythene bag. Once frozen, the bags can be removed from the container, sealed and labelled, then stacked in the freezer.

🌿 To save freezer space, reduce stock right down by rapid boiling, then freeze the concentrated stock in ice-cube trays. To use, drop the ice cubes into a little hot water, then dilute to the desired concentration.

🌿 Soups containing cream, cheese and eggs often do not freeze well, so make the soup without these ingredients and then add them after thawing and reheating the soup.

🌿 When freezing soups in a container, remember to leave some room for the liquid to expand.

Potato soup with watercress

The humble potato makes a hearty soup that cheers the soul in winter. In this delicious version, fresh watercress adds a peppery bite and a super dose of health-giving vitamins.

SERVES 6 · PREP 10 MINUTES · COOK 30 MINUTES

1 tablespoon olive oil

6 spring onions (scallions), thinly sliced

750 g (1½ lb) washed potatoes, peeled and diced

6 cups (1.5 litres/52 fl oz) chicken stock

2 bunches fresh watercress (about 220 g/7 oz in total), tough stalks removed

2 teaspoons bottled horseradish sauce

½ cup (125 g/4 oz) crème fraîche or sour cream

2 tablespoons fresh chives, cut into 2 cm (¾ inch) lengths

1 Heat the olive oil in a large saucepan, then add the spring onions and sauté until softened. Add the potatoes and pour in the stock. Bring to a boil, then reduce the heat and simmer for 15–20 minutes, or until the potatoes are tender.

2 Add the watercress, horseradish sauce and most of the crème fraîche, reserving a little for serving. Stir until the watercress just wilts, being careful not to overcook it.

3 Using a food processor or hand-held blender, process the soup until smooth. Divide among six serving bowls, add a swirl of the remaining crème fraîche, then sprinkle with chives and serve.

For a fresh twist, leave out the horseradish sauce and crème fraîche, and instead stir in 2 teaspoons very finely chopped fresh ginger. Sprinkle the soup with chopped fresh Thai basil and coriander (cilantro) leaves and serve with lime wedges.

Roasted tomato soup

Roasting vegetables enhances their sweetness by concentrating their natural sugars. Red kidney beans make this soup more substantial, with chorizo sausage adding some smoke and spice.

SERVES 4 · PREP 15 MINUTES · COOK 20 MINUTES

1 red onion, unpeeled, quartered

2 red capsicums (bell peppers), halved lengthwise, seeds and membranes removed

4 roma (plum) tomatoes, halved

2 cloves garlic, unpeeled

2 cups (500 ml/17 fl oz) chicken stock

salt and freshly ground black pepper

410 g (13 oz) can red kidney beans, drained and rinsed

100 g (3½ oz) chorizo, diced

2 teaspoons balsamic vinegar

4 tablespoons roughly torn fresh basil leaves

crusty bread, to serve

1 Preheat the grill (broiler) to high. Place the onion, capsicums and tomatoes on a large baking tray, cut sides down, with the garlic cloves.

2 Grill the vegetables for 8 minutes, or until the skins begin to blacken. Place in a clean plastic bag until cool enough to handle, then peel the skins from the onion, capsicums and tomatoes. Squeeze the roasted garlic cloves out of their skins.

3 Chop half the vegetables into small chunks and put the remainder in a food processor or blender with the roasted garlic and stock. Process until smooth, then pour into a saucepan. Add the chopped vegetables and season lightly.

4 Stir in the beans and chorizo, then bring to a boil, stirring occasionally. Reduce the heat, stir in the vinegar, then cover and simmer gently for 2–3 minutes. Toss the basil into the soup just before serving (it will darken if added too soon). Serve with crusty bread.

To save time, use a small jar of roasted red capsicums (bell peppers) and a 410 g (13 oz) can of whole tomatoes. Chop and purée them with the roasted onion and garlic in step 3.

Pasta and noodles

Pasta and noodles are universally popular, quick and easy to cook
and a valuable source of complex carbohydrate. There is an enormous
variety of shapes and types, perfect for any occasion.

Basics

Pasta and noodles are close cousins from other sides of the globe.
Keep them stocked in your pantry and with very little effort
you can enjoy an amazing variety of dishes.

Pasta

Pasta is often simply boiled and tossed with simple, light sauces or rich, chunkier ones, but it can also be stuffed, layered and baked, added to soups, or used in salads.

Cooking pasta

Use 1 tablespoon salt and 6 cups (1.5 litres/52 fl oz) water for each 100 g (3½ oz) of dried pasta, and use a large saucepan, even if you are cooking only a small amount. Cooking the pasta in a large amount of water stops it sticking and brings it back to a boil more quickly – important for a firm yet cooked result.

When cooking fresh pasta you can use about 25 per cent less water because fresh pasta won't expand as much.

If you are cooking pasta for a salad, drain it briefly and quickly toss some olive oil through so it doesn't stick together.

Cooking times will vary greatly depending on the type, so always follow the packet instructions, but test the pasta a few minutes before the given time. Remove a piece of pasta and bite into it. It should be tender, yet still have a slight resistance. Fresh pasta (especially egg pasta such as fettuccine, tagliatelle and lasagne) cooks in just 3–5 minutes. Thin durum wheat pasta (spaghettini, shells, rotini) cooks in 6–9 minutes, and thick durum wheat pasta (penne, spaghetti) in 12–15 minutes.

Types of pasta

Long pasta: Fettucine (long, flat, ribbon-shaped strands); linguine (long, flat ribbon noodles, thinner than fettuccine); pappardelle (thick, flat ribbon noodles about 2 cm/½ inch wide); tagliatelle (long, flat ribbon noodles, like fettuccine but thinner); spaghetti (long, round, string-like strands); spaghettini (thinner spaghetti strands); vermicelli (very thin spaghetti).

Short pasta: Farfalle (bows); conchiglie/cocciole (shell shapes); fusilli/rotini (spirals, twists); orecchiette (small ear shapes).
Tubular pasta: Cannelloni (large round tubes for stuffing); ditali (short tubes); macaroni (smooth, thick tubes); penne (short, smooth tubes, cut diagonally); penne rigati (short, ridged tubes); rigatoni (short, ridged tubes, fatter than penne).
Irregular shapes: Gnocchi (fluted shells); lasagne (flat sheets); ravioli (square-shaped, filled); tortellini (little round shapes, filled); tortelloni (round or rectangular, like ravioli).

Noodles

Noodles are usually made from either wheat or rice flour, and may be dried or pre-cooked. Asian noodles are always disconcertingly long, to symbolise a long and healthy life!

Cooking noodles

Generally, all dried noodles, whether made from rice, wheat or mung bean flour, should be softened by blanching or boiling before cooking. Common types include rice vermicelli (very thin, round, translucent dried noodles); rice stick noodles (flat, translucent dried noodles); and egg noodles (fine or medium, round dried wheat noodles).

Fresh noodles, such as rice stick and wheat noodles, can be cooked straight from the packet.

Vacuum-packed, pre-cooked noodles (also called 'wok-ready' noodles) only need to be heated through when used in a dish. They include hokkien noodles (thick Chinese wheat and egg noodles); Singapore noodles (medium Chinese wheat and egg noodles); and udon (thick, round, Japanese rice noodles).

Hints and tips

Pasta

Shapes and sauces

Thick pasta shapes are best with meat sauces. Long thin pasta, such as spaghetti, goes well with olive oil based sauces that allow the strands to remain separate. If you are layering a dish with a sauce, large flat sheets of lasagne are the obvious choice.

Serving portions

As a general guide, allow about 100 g (3½ oz) of dried pasta, or 150 g (4½ oz) of fresh pasta, per person.

Keeping pasta warm

To keep pasta warm, cover it and place it in a low oven. To reheat pasta, cover it and warm it in a microwave or conventional oven, or in a pan over a low flame with a little added water to stop it sticking together. If you need to keep it for some time, leave a little of the cooking water with it.

Buying and storing pasta

A good Italian brand of dried pasta, made from 100 per cent durum wheat semolina, is often of a superior quality. When buying fresh pasta, check the 'use by' date. Dried pasta, in a tightly closed packet, will keep almost indefinitely in the pantry; fresh pasta must be refrigerated and can only be kept for two or three days (make sure the container is tightly closed). Store any leftover cooked pasta in a tightly closed container in the refrigerator and use within two days.

Quick meals

Keep these pasta basics on hand for quick and tasty meals in moments: dried pasta, extra virgin olive oil, garlic, tomatoes (fresh or canned), fresh and dried herbs, and a hunk of parmesan or other Italian hard cheese.

Noodles

Substitutes

Italian pastas can make good substitutes for egg and wheat flour noodles. The pasta you choose will depend on the shape and thickness of the noodle you are replacing. Thin angel hair pasta can be used to replace cellophane noodles, while fettuccine makes a good substitute for wheat flour noodles.

Buying and storing noodles

Fresh noodles can be stored in their unopened packet in the refrigerator for up to three days. (Check the 'use by' date on the packet before buying.) Fresh noodles can also be frozen: open the packet, divide the noodles into smaller portions and freeze them on a tray. When frozen hard, pack them into freezer boxes or bags so that small quantities can be cooked from frozen as required. With dried noodles, check the 'best before' date when buying, then store as for other types of dried pasta. Once opened, store in an airtight container.

Matching noodles to sauces

Choose a noodle type from the same country as the sauce or topping. For example, use flat Thai rice stick noodles for pad Thai; soba, ramen or udon noodles for Japanese recipes; or hokkien (egg) noodles for Singaporean and Malaysian dishes. Wheat noodles suit dishes from northern China, while rice noodles are more typical of recipes from southern China.

Health tip

Noodles are every bit as nutritious as other types of pasta, with specific benefits depending on the grain from which they are made. Many non-wheat noodles are gluten-free, which makes them suitable for people who have a wheat or gluten intolerance. Remember that crispy noodles, popular in many restaurant dishes, absorb a lot of oil during deep-frying, so it's best to enjoy them now and again rather than every day.

Pappardelle with chicken

Pappardelle is the widest of the ribbon pastas. If you can't find it, tagliatelle or linguine will work equally well. Chicken, cherry tomatoes and rocket complement each other beautifully here.

SERVES 4 • PREP 10 MINUTES • COOK 15 MINUTES

2 tablespoons olive oil
1 red onion, halved and thinly sliced
2 cloves garlic, crushed
450 g (1 lb) boneless, skinless chicken breasts, cut into 2 cm (¾ inch) cubes
400 g (12½ oz) cherry tomatoes, halved
400 g (12½ oz) pappardelle
150 g (4½ oz) rocket (arugula)
salt and freshly ground black pepper

1 Heat the olive oil in a frying pan with a lid. Add the onion and garlic and gently sauté for 2 minutes. Add the chicken and stir-fry over medium heat until lightly coloured, then reduce the heat slightly and stir in the tomatoes. Cover and simmer, stirring occasionally, for 8–10 minutes, or until the tomatoes are very soft and the chicken is cooked through.

2 Meanwhile, cook the pasta in a large saucepan of salted boiling water, following the packet instructions. Drain and keep warm if necessary.

3 Stir the rocket into the chicken mixture and season to taste. Put the pasta in a large warmed serving bowl. Spoon the chicken mixture over and toss gently to combine. Serve immediately.

Capers, bacon, pancetta, olives, cheese and many canned ingredients (including tomatoes, anchovies and tuna) can be quite salty. If using such ingredients in a pasta sauce, don't add extra salt during cooking. Taste the finished sauce, then adjust the seasoning if necessary.

Pad Thai

The Thai word 'pad' is used to describe stir-fried food.
Tamarind paste adds a fruity, tart sweetness to this dish.

SERVES 4 • PREP 15 MINUTES • COOK 10 MINUTES

185 g (6 oz) rice stick noodles
80 ml (3½ fl oz) peanut oil
2 spring onions (scallions), finely chopped
2 cloves garlic, finely chopped
2 large eggs, beaten
2 tablespoons fish sauce
2 tablespoons tamarind paste
2 teaspoons sugar
2 tablespoons lime juice
2 tablespoons tomato sauce (ketchup)
16 large raw prawns (shrimp), peeled
    and deveined, tails left on
¼ cup (40 g/1½ oz) chopped roasted peanuts
100 g (3½ oz) bean sprouts, trimmed
3 tablespoons fresh coriander (cilantro)
3 tablespoons fresh Thai basil
lime wedges, to serve

1 Place the noodles in a heatproof bowl and cover with boiling water. Leave to stand for 10–15 minutes, or until soft.

2 Meanwhile, heat the peanut oil in a wok or large frying pan. Add the spring onions and stir-fry for 1 minute, or until softened. Add the garlic and cook for 30 seconds. Pour in the eggs and stir until lightly cooked. Add the fish sauce, tamarind paste, sugar, lime juice and tomato sauce and mix until well combined.

3 Drain the softened noodles and add to the wok, tossing them through the sauce.

4 Add the prawns and cook for 2–3 minutes, or until the prawns turn pink. Remove the pan from the heat, then add the peanuts, sprouts, coriander and basil. Toss gently and serve with lime wedges.

Rice noodles are a common ingredient in East and Southeast Asian cooking. Available dried, frozen and fresh, they vary in width from very fine vermicelli to sheets of dough. They are transparent and have a gelatinous, chewy texture.

Rice, beans and grains

Very economical and highly nutritious, these invaluable pantry items are tasty alternatives to potatoes or pasta and play an important role in a balanced diet. With so many different varieties to choose from, you'll never be short of a satisfying meal.

Basics

Many strains of rice and literally hundreds of varieties of beans are grown all over the world — adzuki, black-eyed, cannellini, kidney, pinto and soybeans, to name just a few. Barley, buckwheat, maize, millet, oats, quinoa, rye, spelt and wheat are the most common types of grains.

Absorption method

To cook long-grain white rice by this method, you need about twice the volume of water to rice. Put the rice and water in a heavy-based saucepan and bring to a boil. When the water is boiling, turn the heat down to low so the water is very gently simmering. Stir with a fork and put the lid on. Leave to cook, covered, for 10–15 minutes (check the packet instructions).

To test if the rice is ready, lift out a few grains on a fork. If the rice still seems too firm but all the water has been absorbed, add a little more boiling water and simmer for a few more minutes. When the rice is tender, remove the pan from the heat and set aside to rest for a few minutes. This will allow the rice to absorb any last traces of water. (The rice will retain its heat if you keep the lid on; you can also slip a clean tea towel/ dish towel between the pan and the lid to help dry out the rice.) Finally, fluff up the rice lightly with a fork to separate the grains, then serve.

Wholegrain long-grain rices (brown rice, wild rice and red rice) can also be cooked by the absorption method, but you will need more water (2½ times the volume of water to rice) and longer cooking. Brown basmati rice takes about 25 minutes; other long-grain brown rices, wild rice and red rice need about 30–40 minutes cooking.

Microwaving

Measure one part rice to two parts water and place in a microwave-proof bowl. Rest the lid lightly on top and cook the rice for 12 minutes. Leave to stand for 5 minutes, still covered, then stir before serving.

Boiling

Rice can be cooked in a large volume of fast-boiling water. Allow 10–15 minutes for white rice and 30–35 minutes for brown rice. Check for tenderness towards the end of cooking time, as overcooking will result in mushy, tasteless rice. When the rice is tender, drain it in a sieve.

If you use more than one type of rice in the kitchen, experiment to find the exact proportion of rice, water and cooking time that works for each variety as they all have different absorption qualities.

Cooking whole grains

Whole grains can be cooked like rice. Whole rye grains need to be soaked in cold water overnight before cooking. Whole-wheat grains, if not pre-cooked, can be soaked overnight to shorten the cooking time. Allow about 75 g (2½ oz) per person.

After soaking, measure out three parts water to one part grain (millet needs four parts water). Pour the water into a saucepan with a tight-fitting lid and bring to a boil, then add the grains and return to the boil. Lower the heat and simmer very gently, without stirring, until all the water has been absorbed. The cooking times will vary from grain to grain: millet and quinoa will usually be tender in about 20 minutes; tougher grains may take an hour or more. Remove from the heat and leave, with the lid on, for a further 10 minutes. By this time the grains should be separate and tender but not mushy. Fluff up lightly with a fork and serve.

Hints and tips

Know your grains

Couscous is made from grains of semolina given a coating of extra fine flour so that they absorb moisture more easily. It is delicious with North African dishes.

Polenta is a traditional Italian staple made with cornmeal (ground maize) and can be coarsely or finely ground. Instant polenta takes only 5 minutes to prepare, and is a tasty substitute for mashed potato.

Quinoa is a grain-like seed from South America. Used as an alternative to rice, it is a rich source of protein and nutrients.

Wild rice is not, in fact, rice but a type of grass. It is gluten-free and needs a longer cooking time than rice.

Calculating quantities

As a general guide, 1 cup white rice makes 3 cups cooked; 1 cup brown rice makes 2 cups cooked. As an accompaniment, allow 60–90 g (2–3 oz) uncooked rice per person. Where rice is the main ingredient, allow about 125 g (4 oz) per person.

Soaking and boiling beans

Lentils and split peas don't need soaking, but most dried beans and peas should be soaked for at least 8 hours. They have been soaked long enough if there is no wrinkling on the skin and the beans look plump and have increased in size, sometimes up to three times the original size. After soaking, drain and rinse. Discard the soaking water and use fresh water for cooking. (Do not salt the cooking water, because this may toughen the beans and prolong the cooking time.)

A 10–15 minute fast boil at the start of cooking will remove toxins from dried beans and peas. After the fast boil, reduce the heat so the liquid is just simmering. Skim the froth from the surface, then partly cover the pan and leave to cook gently until the beans are tender, topping up with more boiling water as necessary. Follow the packet instructions for cooking times.

Unsticking cooked rice grains

Transfer the rice to a large sieve and rinse it thoroughly over the sink with boiling water. Shake off the excess liquid, return the rice to the cleaned saucepan, cover and leave for 5 minutes. Remove the lid, fluff up the grains with a fork and serve.

Storing cooked rice

Cooked rice can be stored in a covered container in the refrigerator for up to two days or in the freezer for up to three months. Always keep it refrigerated or frozen, or it could develop toxins that cause food poisoning. Reheat the rice, loosely covered, in a steamer or microwave.

Making a basic risotto

Simmer 4 cups (1 litre/35 fl oz) vegetable stock in a small pan. In a large saucepan, sauté 1 chopped onion and 1 crushed garlic clove in 1 tablespoon olive oil over medium heat for 5 minutes, or until softened. With a wooden spoon, stir in 1½ cups (300 g/9½ oz) arborio rice. Add 150 ml (5 fl oz) dry white wine and simmer until almost evaporated. Add a ladleful of hot stock and stir until the stock has been absorbed. Continue adding the hot stock a ladleful at a time, stirring for about 20 minutes, until the risotto is tender and creamy. Stir in 2 tablespoons chopped fresh parsley or chives, season with freshly ground black pepper and serve.

Tips for perfect risotto

Simmer the stock in another pot while cooking the rice, so the temperature of the rice never drops. Use arborio rice, and 'toast' it in the hot oil before adding your hot stock. Add the stock gradually, so each ladleful is fully absorbed before adding more, preventing mushy rice. Stir almost constantly – at the end of cooking, it should be creamy and tender, but with a firm centre.

Fried rice

Spiced with garlic, sesame, ginger and chilli, this tempting dish is a variation on the Indonesian classic 'Nasi goreng'. A meal in itself, it's perfect for a relaxed lunch as much of it can be prepared ahead.

SERVES 4 • PREP 25 MINUTES + 30 MINUTES MARINATING • COOK 10 MINUTES

2 teaspoons sesame oil

2 teaspoons sherry vinegar

2 tablespoons salt-reduced soy sauce

250 g (8 oz) lean rump or fillet steak, cut across the grain into thin strips

1¾ cups (350 g/12 oz) long-grain white rice

2 eggs

3 spring onions (scallions), sliced on the diagonal

2 tablespoons chopped fresh coriander (cilantro)

salt and freshly ground black pepper

2½ tablespoons vegetable oil

8 raw prawns (shrimp), peeled and deveined, tails left on

2 cloves garlic, crushed

1 green chilli, seeded and thinly sliced

1 tablespoon grated fresh ginger

2 carrots, peeled and roughly grated

1 cup (150 g/5½ oz) frozen peas, thawed

splash of chilli sauce (optional)

1 In a bowl, whisk the sesame oil, vinegar and half the soy sauce. Add the beef, toss to coat, then cover and refrigerate for at least 30 minutes, or overnight.

2 Meanwhile, cook the rice in lightly salted boiling water for 12 minutes, or until almost tender. Drain, rinse with boiling water, then spread out on a tray and leave to cool. (For best results, cool the rice overnight.)

3 Beat the eggs in a small bowl, stir in the spring onions and coriander and season. Heat 2 teaspoons of the oil in a non-stick frying pan and pour in the eggs. Cook for a few seconds, then stir gently with a fork for 1 minute, or until the base begins to set. Stop stirring and cook for a further 2 minutes, or until lightly set. Roll up the omelette and keep warm.

4 Heat half the remaining oil in a wok until hot. Add the beef and marinade and brown over high heat for 1 minute. Remove with a slotted spoon and set aside.

5 Add the remaining oil to the wok. Stir-fry the prawns, garlic, chilli and ginger for 2 minutes, then add the carrots, peas and rice and toss for 1 minute. Add the beef and remaining soy sauce and toss until hot.

6 Spoon the rice mixture into warmed bowls. Cut the omelette into thin strips and scatter over the rice. Serve with chilli sauce if desired.

Burghul with spring vegetables

Burghul is a source of complex carbohydrates, protein, insoluble fibre and vitamin E, which are all essential for good health. Adding some spring vegetables into the mix makes a bowl of nature's bounty.

SERVES 6 · PREP 15 MINUTES + 30 MINUTES SOAKING · COOK 10 MINUTES

1¼ cups (225 g/8 oz) burghul (bulgur)
2 tablespoons olive oil
3 tablespoons lemon juice
1 teaspoon salt
½ teaspoon freshly ground black pepper
2 leeks, white part only, cut in half lengthwise,
    then into 2 cm (¾ inch) pieces
2 cloves garlic, crushed
12 asparagus spears, cut into 5 cm (2 inch) lengths
1 cup (150 g/5 oz) frozen peas, thawed
3 tablespoons chopped fresh mint

1 Put the burghul in a large heatproof bowl and pour 3½ cups (875 ml/30 fl oz) boiling water over. Leave to soak for 15 minutes, then stir. Allow to stand for another 15 minutes, or until the burghul is soft. Drain through a large, fine-meshed sieve to remove any remaining liquid.

2 In a large bowl, whisk 1 tablespoon of the olive oil with the lemon juice, salt and black pepper. Add the burghul and fluff with a fork.

3 Heat the remaining oil in a frying pan over low heat. Add the leeks and garlic and sauté for 5 minutes, or until the leeks are tender. Add to the burghul mixture.

4 In a steamer set over a pan of boiling water, steam the asparagus for 4 minutes, or until tender, adding the peas during the final 30 seconds. Add to the burghul mixture with the mint and toss to combine. Serve at room temperature or chilled.

Did you know burghul is made from parboiled wheat kernels that have been dried and cracked? Traditionally used for tabouleh and other salads, burghul is also good for stuffings and pilafs.

RICE, BEANS AND GRAINS

Eggs and dairy

Eggs and milk are essentials in most kitchens. Such versatile ingredients,
they are indispensable in a wide range of recipes, and have many health benefits.
Butter, cheese and cream, being rich in fat, are some of life's little indulgences.

Basics

A simple, perfect egg makes a glorious breakfast or simple meal when dished up with some love and respect. And there's no end to what you can do once you've mastered the knack of a good basic white sauce and creamy custard!

Scrambling eggs

Crack the eggs into a bowl, add 1 tablespoon milk per egg and salt and pepper to taste. Whisk well. Melt a small knob of butter in a non-stick saucepan over medium heat. Pour in the eggs and cook, stirring often, until they are almost set but still soft and glossy. Quickly remove from the heat, as the eggs will keep cooking – don't overcook or they will become dry and grainy.

Boiling eggs

Put a room-temperature egg in a saucepan with tepid water to cover. Bring to a boil, reduce the heat and simmer for 3–4 minutes for a soft-boiled egg, and 7 minutes for hard-boiled. Remove with a slotted spoon. If the egg is soft-boiled, remove the 'cap' or top of the shell straight away, to arrest the cooking process. Place hard-boiled eggs in a bowl of cold water to cool before peeling.

Poaching eggs

Fill a deep frying pan with 4 cm (1¼ inches) water and bring to a simmer. Add 1 teaspoon vinegar. Carefully break the eggs into the water and poach for about 3 minutes – the whites should be set, and the yolks still a bit runny. Near the end of cooking, baste the yolks with the simmering water. Lift out with a slotted spoon.

Making an omelette

Whisk 2 eggs in a bowl with 1 tablespoon cold water and salt and pepper to taste. Melt a small knob of butter in a non-stick frying pan over high heat, swirling to coat the pan. When the butter is foaming, add the eggs. After a few seconds, tilt the pan and use a spatula to draw the cooked egg into the centre, so the uncooked egg can run onto the pan. Continue tilting the pan and drawing the cooked egg in, to build up a plump omelette. When there is very little runny egg left, add a filling such as grated cheese, diced tomatoes or cooked vegetables, then leave undisturbed for 10 seconds so the omelette can set and become golden underneath. Remove from the heat and use the spatula to fold one-third of the omelette over towards the centre. Slide the omelette across the pan, onto a serving plate.

Basic white sauce

Melt 50 g (2 oz) butter in a heavy-based saucepan over low heat. Remove from the heat and stir in ⅓ cup (50 g/1½ oz) plain (all-purpose) flour until smooth. Slowly add 2 cups (500 ml/17 fl oz) milk, stirring or whisking constantly. Return to the heat and bring to a boil, still stirring or whisking. Reduce the heat and simmer gently for 5 minutes, stirring occasionally. Season with salt and ground white pepper and use immediately. Serves 4.

Custard

In a bowl, beat 4 egg yolks, 4 teaspoons cornflour (cornstarch) and 4 tablespoons caster (superfine) sugar until smooth. Pour 2 cups (500 ml/17 fl oz) milk into a saucepan and bring to a boil, then slowly pour it onto the egg yolk mixture, stirring thoroughly. Return the mixture to the saucepan and cook over low heat, stirring constantly, until it thickens to a custard consistency. Remove from the heat and strain into a bowl. Serve hot or cold. Serves 4.

Hints and tips

Buying and storing eggs

Check the 'best before' date on egg cartons; this is usually three weeks after the egg was laid. You can refrigerate eggs for up to three weeks, but keep them in their cartons and away from possible contaminants such as raw meat and poultry.

Checking eggs for freshness

Check uncooked eggs for freshness by putting them in a bowl of cold water. A fresh egg stays at the bottom of the bowl, while a stale egg floats. If it lies horizontally at the bottom it is very fresh; if it begins to point upwards it is about a week old; if it stands vertically it is stale. A fresh egg tends to feel heavy in the hand.

Very fresh eggs give the best results when poaching and frying, and are also a better choice for soft-boiling, omelettes, scrambling and general cooking. However, very fresh eggs (only a few days old) are not ideal for hard-boiling, as the shell (and the membrane just underneath it) will be hard to peel off. For hard-boiling, eggs that are one to two weeks old are best.

Storing cheese

Ideally, cheese should be stored in the refrigerator at a temperature of 4–6°C (39–43°F). Keep cheese in its own container or separate compartment and consume within two weeks. Soft, unripened cheeses – such as cottage cheese, fromage frais, mozzarella, ricotta and cream cheese – should be eaten as soon as possible after purchase.

Melted cheese toppings

Don't overcook grilled or baked cheese toppings – cheese only needs to be melted. Once it reaches 75°C (165°F) it can become hard or chewy, so don't put it too close to a fierce grill (broiler). For a delicious result, try adding an equal quantity of fresh breadcrumbs to grated cheese.

Types of milk and cream

Different milk varieties have different names around the world. In some countries full-cream milk is called whole milk, while both skimmed and semi-skimmed milk may be known as skim milk. Skim milk has less fat than low-fat milk, and various types of low- or non-fat milk are available. Generally, unless a recipe specifies otherwise, full-cream (whole) milk is intended.

Confusingly, there are even more names for cream. 'Thick', 'heavy' or 'double' cream is cream that is high in fat. As it can be boiled, it is used in sauces to enrich them, but it can also be whipped to a soft or firm consistency, so it is also sometimes called 'whipping' cream.

'Pure', 'light' or 'single' cream cannot be whipped, but is good for pouring or for using in cooking when you want a richer texture or flavour than milk will give. In some recipes it is referred to as 'pouring' cream.

Freezing milk and cream

Milk can be frozen in waxed cartons or plastic containers that allow enough room for expansion (for this reason, don't use glass bottles). You can freeze milk for up to one month, then thaw it slowly in the refrigerator.

Cream that has a milk fat content of 35 per cent or more can also be frozen. Best results are achieved by half-whipping the cream before freezing it.

Making homemade yogurt

Bring 600 ml (21 fl oz) milk (skim or full fat, depending on how creamy you like your yogurt) to a boil, then allow to cool to blood temperature (37°C/98°F on a kitchen thermometer). Stir in 1 tablespoon plain live yogurt, then pour into a bowl or wide-necked flask. Cover and leave in a warm place for 8–12 hours to set, then refrigerate. For thick, creamy yogurt, drain it in a sieve lined with muslin (cheesecloth).

Thyme and oregano soufflés

Individual soufflés never fail to impress. The fruit chutney base is a surprise extra that complements the herbs.

SERVES 4 · PREP 20 MINUTES + 10 MINUTES COOLING · COOK 30 MINUTES

olive oil, for greasing
3 tablespoons butter
2 tablespoons plain (all-purpose) flour
1⅓ cups (330 ml/11 fl oz) milk
1 cup (100 g/3½ oz) grated strong cheddar
¼ teaspoon cayenne pepper
4 large eggs, separated
2 teaspoons finely chopped fresh thyme
2 teaspoons finely chopped fresh oregano
2 tablespoons finely chopped fresh parsley
2 tablespoons fruit chutney

1 Preheat the oven to 200°C (400°F/Gas 6). Lightly oil four 1 cup (250 ml/9 fl oz) ramekins.

2 Meanwhile, melt the butter in a small saucepan over low heat. Using a wooden spoon, fold in the flour, stirring continuously for about 1 minute. Remove the pan from the heat and gradually add the milk, stirring until smooth. Place back over medium heat and stir until the mixture thickens and thickly coats the back of the spoon.

3 Fold in the cheese and cayenne pepper, then transfer to a large bowl, cover with plastic wrap and leave to cool. When the mixture has cooled, stir the egg yolks and herbs through.

4 In a clean, small bowl, beat the egg whites until soft peaks form. Lightly fold them into the soufflé mixture, just until white streaks are no longer visible – take care not to overmix.

5 Place ½ tablespoon chutney in each ramekin. Divide the soufflé mixture among the ramekins, taking care not to mix in the chutney. Run a small spatula around the rims to shape the tops. Place the ramekins on a baking tray and bake for 20 minutes, or until the soufflés are risen and golden. Serve at once.

Herb butters

Spread these delicious butters on crusty bread, or use them to dress up cooked vegetables and barbecued meat.

SERVES 10–12 • PREP 10 MINUTES EACH • COOK 0–2 MINUTES

Coriander and chilli butter

¼ cup (40 g/1½ oz) macadamia nuts,
    roughly chopped
250 g (8 oz) butter, softened
3 tablespoons chopped fresh coriander (cilantro)
2 fresh makrut (kaffir lime) leaves, finely chopped
1 large red chilli, finely diced
1 tablespoon lime juice

1   Toast the nuts in a dry frying pan over medium heat, tossing until the smallest pieces are just golden. Transfer to a small bowl and leave to cool.

2   Put the butter in a bowl. Add the macadamias and remaining ingredients and mix well.

3   Place the mixture on a sheet of plastic wrap about 20 cm (8 inches) long. Roll into a log about 5 cm (2 inches) in diameter, then wrap tightly and chill until required.

Sage butter

250 g (8 oz) butter, softened
1 tablespoon finely chopped fresh sage
3 tablespoons finely chopped fresh flat-leaf
    parsley
10 pitted green olives, roughly chopped
2 anchovy fillets, finely chopped

1   Put the butter in a bowl. Add the remaining ingredients and mix well.

2   Place the mixture on a sheet of plastic wrap about 20 cm (8 inches) long. Roll into a log about 5 cm (2 inches) in diameter, then wrap tightly and chill until required.

Herb butters are so versatile! Try the following combinations:
❧ some chopped fresh parsley, grated lemon zest and a splash of lemon juice;
❧ 125 g (4 oz) blue cheese and some chopped fresh chives, mint and dill;
❧ a big dollop of horseradish cream, a tablespoon of dijon mustard and some chopped fresh parsley.

Meat

*Beef, veal, lamb and pork are excellent sources of protein.
Each meat has its own distinctive taste and texture, and comes in
a wonderful variety of cuts. By picking the best methods of preparing
and cooking the different cuts, you can bring out their best qualities.*

Basics

The golden rule of meat cookery is to never overcook your meat or it will be tough and dry. If in doubt, it's better to slightly undercook it: you can always cook it a little longer until it's done to perfection!

Calculating portions

Allow approximately 125 g (4 oz) of lean meat per person, and about 250 g (8 oz) for cuts with the bone in.

Cuts of meat

In general, cheaper cuts of meat are tougher than prime cuts and are best suited to gentle, slow, moist cooking methods, such as pot-roasting, braising and stewing. They may also be marinated before cooking to tenderise them. Just because they are cheaper, however, does not mean these cuts are inferior. Indeed, with long, slow cooking these tougher cuts of meat become mouthwateringly tender – gourmet on a budget!

Tender cuts are more suitable for quicker cooking methods over more intense heat, such as grilling, barbecuing and frying. More expensive cuts of meat may be 'stretched' to go further, for example by stuffing a boned joint, or by supplementing the meat with grains or vegetables.

Marinating meat

Pour 1 cup (250 ml/9 fl oz) wine (use dry red wine for beef or lamb, and dry white wine for pork) into a mixing bowl. Add 2 tablespoons olive oil, 1 tablespoon lemon juice, 1 small chopped onion, 1 peeled and sliced carrot, 1 chopped celery stalk, 1–2 cloves crushed garlic, 1 bouquet garni (made by tying together some bay leaves and a few sprigs of rosemary, parsley and thyme) and 6 black peppercorns. Mix together, pour into a shallow non-metal dish and add your choice of meat. Gently toss the meat to coat it in the marinade, then cover and refrigerate for several hours or overnight, turning it now and then.

Resting meat

Always rest a roast before carving it. This relaxes the meat fibres and allows the juices to be reabsorbed, thereby enhancing the tenderness of the meat. To do this simply remove the roast from the pan, place on a warmed plate and cover loosely with foil. Leave for 10–15 minutes while you make the gravy.

Making gravy

Take the roasted meat out of the roasting tin (baking pan) and set it aside to rest (see above).

Drain away a little of the fat from the pan, leaving about 1 tablespoon of fat and the brown residue from the roast meat. Place the roasting tin (baking pan) on the stovetop over medium heat. Bring the pan juices to a boil, then add 4 tablespoons plain (all-purpose) flour and stir until no lumps remain. Reduce the heat a little and cook, stirring constantly, until the flour mixture is well browned – take care that it doesn't burn.

Take the roasting tin (baking pan) off the heat and slowly pour in 3½ cups (875 ml/30 fl oz) stock, stirring until smooth. Return to the heat and bring the mixture to a boil, then reduce the heat and simmer for 3 minutes, stirring often. Season to taste and serve.

Tips for enriching pan gravy

To enrich pan gravy, try using half wine and half stock. (First reduce the wine or alcohol by rapid boiling to eliminate any harsh flavours.) A splash of worcestershire or soy sauce gives great flavour and colour, while tomato paste (concentrated purée) will add colour and richness. Just before serving, stir in finely chopped fresh herbs such as parsley or chives.

Hints and tips

Stewing, braising, casseroling and pot-roasting

☙ These are slow, moist methods of cooking at low temperatures, either in the oven or on the stovetop. They help to tenderise the more coarsely grained cuts of meat.

☙ To get the best flavour, use a well-flavoured stock and/or wine, cider or beer, as well as herbs and spices.

☙ Add lots of vegetables for extra interest and nutrition. You can even add rice or pasta near the end of cooking.

☙ For a meal-in-a-pot, when cooking a casserole or stew in the oven, top it with a thick layer of sliced potatoes about an hour before the end of cooking time. Bake without the lid on so the potatoes become crisp and golden brown.

Roasting

☙ To help keep a boned joint in a nice shape and ensure it cooks evenly, tie it with string.

☙ Place the meat on a rack in a roasting tin (baking pan) so that the largest cut surfaces are exposed and any fat sits on the top. As the fat melts during roasting it will baste the meat.

☙ If the meat is very lean, baste it with the hot fat in the roasting tin from time to time during cooking. Alternatively, cover the joint with foil.

☙ The most accurate test for doneness is by checking the internal temperature with a meat thermometer.

Roasting times and temperatures

☙ The cooking time for roasting meat is based on the weight of the joint. The ideal temperature for roasting is 180°C (350°F).

Beef and lamb: rare 20 minutes per 500 g (1 lb) plus 20 minutes; medium 25 minutes per 500 g (1 lb) plus 25 minutes; well done 30 minutes per 500 g (1 lb) plus 30 minutes.

Veal: well done 30 minutes per 500 g (1 lb) plus 30 minutes.

Pork: medium 30 minutes per 500 g (1 lb) plus 30 minutes; well done 35 minutes per 500 g (1 lb) plus 35 minutes.

Grilling (broiling)

☙ Grilling (broiling) involves cooking meat on a rack under an oven grill (broiler). Any fat will drip into the grill pan below.

☙ Always preheat your grill, and brush a little oil over the meat before grilling it, or baste it during cooking. You can also add moisture by marinating the meat beforehand.

☙ Watch the heat: if the heat is too fierce and the meat too near it, the meat will be browned before the inside is cooked.

Chargrilling

☙ A quick, healthy cooking method needing very little oil. Lean cuts of meat are seared in a ridged cast-iron grill pan over high heat on the stovetop, giving the meat charred stripes.

☙ Use a chargrill pan with a thick base – the heavier the better.

☙ Heat the chargrill pan thoroughly before you put in the meat, usually for 10 minutes.

☙ Chargrilling causes smoke, so turn the extractor fan on high.

Barbecuing

☙ Use the barbecue to cook steaks, chops, cutlets, sausages, homemade burgers and kebabs, as well as larger pieces of meat such as a butterflied whole leg of lamb.

☙ When barbecuing steak, preheat the barbecue plate to medium–high. Brush both sides of the steak with olive oil so it won't stick to the plate, and only turn it once during cooking, or the juices will escape and the meat will be tough.

Barbecuing and grilling times

For steak 1.5 cm (½ inch) thick: rare 1–1½ minutes on each side; medium 2–3 minutes on each side; well done 3–4 minutes on each side.

For steak 2–3 cm (1 inch) thick: rare 2–3 minutes on each side; medium 4–5 minutes on each side; well done 5–6 minutes on each side.

Belgian potato hotpot

Seriously robust fare, and so very easy to prepare! Lazily throw it all together on a slow weekend afternoon and let the oven do all the work, filling the home with enticing aromas all the way to dinnertime.

SERVES 4–6 • PREP 35 MINUTES • COOK 2 HOURS 15 MINUTES

1 kg (2 lb) piece of roasting beef (beef chuck)
salt and freshly ground black pepper
100 g (3½ oz) bacon, chopped
3–4 small onions, cut into wedges
5 sprigs fresh thyme
2 dried bay leaves
1 cup (250 ml/9 fl oz) dry red wine
½ cup (125 ml/4 fl oz) beef stock
750 g (1½ lb) small boiling (waxy) or all-purpose
    potatoes, peeled and sliced
4 carrots, peeled and sliced

1 Remove the sinews and fat from the beef, then rinse the meat under cold running water. Pat dry with paper towel and rub on all sides with a little salt and black pepper.

2 Fry the bacon in a flameproof casserole dish or heavy-based saucepan over high heat without any oil. Add the beef and brown thoroughly on all sides. Add the onions and fry until well browned, stirring constantly. Sprinkle the leaves from four of the thyme sprigs over the beef and place the bay leaves and remaining thyme sprig on top.

3 Pour in the wine and stir to loosen the solids from the bottom of the dish. Heat the stock in a separate pan, then pour into the dish. Cover and simmer over low heat for 90 minutes, turning the beef occasionally. Season the sauce generously with salt and black pepper.

4 Add the potatoes and carrots, then cover and simmer for a further 30 minutes, or until the vegetables are soft.

5 Discard the bay leaves and thyme sprig. Remove the meat to a chopping board, carve into slices, then place back in the dish. Season to taste and serve hot from the pot.

Lamb with herb and garlic rub

Lamb is best teamed with herbs that pack a punch, as this trio does. Also try a combination of oregano, thyme and mint or coriander.

SERVES 6 • PREP 20 MINUTES + 1 HOUR MARINATING • COOK 2 HOURS

2 kg (4 lb) leg of lamb
juice of 1 lemon

Herb and garlic rub
3 tablespoons finely chopped fresh thyme
2 tablespoons finely chopped fresh rosemary
2 tablespoons finely chopped fresh parsley
8 cloves garlic, finely chopped
1 tablespoon sea salt flakes
½ teaspoon freshly ground black pepper
¼ cup (60 ml/2 fl oz) olive oil

1 To make the herb and garlic rub, mix the herbs, garlic, sea salt and black pepper in a bowl. Pour in the olive oil and mix until well combined.

2 Using a sharp knife, make several slits about 5 mm (¼ inch) deep over the lamb. Rub the herb and garlic mixture all over the meat, pushing it into the slits. Cover the lamb loosely with foil and leave to marinate at room temperature for 1 hour.

3 Preheat the oven to 180°C (350°F/Gas 4). Place the lamb on a roasting tin (baking tray), fat side up, and roast for 1 hour. Cover with foil and cook for a further 1 hour, or until done to your liking.

4 Transfer the lamb to a cutting board and sprinkle with the lemon juice. Cover loosely with foil and leave to rest for 10–15 minutes before carving. Serve with roasted vegetables.

It is important to rest a joint of meat for at least 10 minutes before carving and serving. When rested, the internal and external temperatures even out and the juices are redistributed, making the meat more succulent and easier to carve.

Poultry

Few can resist a golden, tender roast chicken: for many it's the ultimate comfort food! Chicken is wonderfully versatile, and offers lean protein plus essential vitamins and minerals, like its cousins turkey, pigeon, quail and guinea fowl. Duck and goose, with their rich dark meat, are also deeply delicious.

Basics

Buy the best bird you can afford: although free-range and organic poultry is more expensive, the taste is far superior to battery-reared birds. Corn-fed chickens have a yellowish flesh and a good, slightly gamey taste.

Perfect roast chicken

Preheat the oven to 220°C (425°F/Gas 7). Wipe the cavity of a 2 kg (4 lb) free-range chicken with paper towel and place a quartered lemon and 6 thyme sprigs inside. (Alternatively, replace the thyme with stuffing; see recipe below. If using stuffing, increase the roasting time by about 20 minutes.) Tie the legs together with kitchen string and tuck the neck flap and wings underneath. In a small bowl mix 3 tablespoons softened butter with 2 tablespoons olive oil and brush all over the chicken. Place the chicken on a rack in a roasting tin (baking pan), breast side down. Roast for 30 minutes, then turn the chicken breast side up and baste well. Arrange 500 g (1 lb) par-boiled new potatoes around the chicken, reduce the oven temperature to 180°C (350°F/Gas 4) and roast for a further 40–50 minutes, or until the juices run clear when tested in the thickest part with a skewer. Remove from the oven, cover loosely with foil and allow to rest for 10 minutes before carving. Serves 6.

Stuffing recipe

Gently heat 2 tablespoons butter and 1 tablespoon olive oil in a large frying pan over medium heat. Sauté 1 finely chopped onion and 2 finely chopped celery stalks for 10 minutes or until soft, then tip into a bowl. Stir in 1¼ cups (100 g/3½ oz) fresh white breadcrumbs, 1 tablespoon chopped fresh mixed herbs (such as thyme, sage, parsley and tarragon) or 2 teaspoons dried mixed herbs. Add 1 beaten egg, season with salt and freshly ground black pepper and mix well to bind the mixture together. Allow to cool completely, then loosely stuff the chicken, pushing the stuffing well up inside the cavity to make a neat shape, before tying the legs together.

Testing for doneness

To test if a roast chicken is cooked, pierce the thigh joint with a skewer. The juices should run clear. Alternatively, use a cooking thermometer. At the end of the recommended cooking time, insert the thermometer probe into the thickest part of the meat. For chicken and turkey, the internal temperature of the dark thigh meat should be at least 75°C (170°F); the white meat of the breast should have reached 71°C (160°F).

Basic chicken stir-fry

Heat 2 tablespoons olive oil in a large non-stick frying pan over medium–high heat. Add 500 g (1 lb) boneless, skinless chicken breast fillets, cut into thin strips. Sauté for 4 minutes, or until barely cooked through. Sprinkle with ¼ teaspoon salt and ¼ teaspoon freshly ground black pepper and remove from the pan. In the same pan, sauté some sliced vegetables such as capsicum (bell pepper) and zucchini (courgette) for 4 minutes, or until just tender. Add ¼ teaspoon salt and 2 crushed garlic cloves and sauté for 30 seconds. Add 10 halved cherry tomatoes and ½ teaspoon dried oregano and sauté for a further minute. Return the chicken to the pan, add 2 teaspoons balsamic vinegar and toss until heated through. Serves 4.

A world of flavours

Cooks in every country have inventive ways with poultry and game. The Spanish adore it in a saffron-spiced paella; in the Middle East it's paired with exotic pomegranates and walnuts, and in Mexico with chilli and chocolate mole sauce! When cooking birds, countless herbs and spices are at your disposal.

Hints and tips

For successful roasting

🌿 There is no need to rinse chicken – the skin has natural oils that keep it moist during cooking.

🌿 If using a fan-forced oven, your cooking time may be a little quicker, so start checking your dish a little earlier.

🌿 Customise recipes to suit your own tastes. Rub the skin of the bird with your favourite herbs or spices to create your own signature dish.

🌿 Roasting a chicken will take approximately 20 minutes for every 500 g (1 lb) of weight. Overcooking your chicken will cause it to dry out. Frozen birds may have added water, which will drain out as the meat thaws, so weigh after thawing to calculate the cooking time.

🌿 To roast vegetables such as potatoes, carrots and onions with your chicken, add them to the roasting tin (baking pan) after the bird has been in the oven for 30–40 minutes.

🌿 To test if the chicken is done, insert a skewer into the thickest part of the thigh. If the juices run clear with no sign of pink, the chicken is cooked.

🌿 When the chicken is cooked, remove it from the oven and loosely cover it with foil. Set aside for 10–15 minutes to rest before carving it to allow the juices to settle.

🌿 To serve a roast chicken, carve the breast meat into long thin slices, then remove the legs with the thighs and cut them in half at the joint.

Tips on stuffing

🌿 Only stuff a chicken or turkey just before cooking, otherwise the stuffing may become contaminated from the raw juices from the bird.

🌿 To make breadcrumbs for stuffings, remove the crusts from day-old bread and finely chop the bread in a food processor.

🌿 Try adding different herbs to the stuffing (parsley, rosemary, oregano or basil are good).

🌿 Before storing a cooked chicken, remove the stuffing.

Serving sizes

🌿 When buying a whole turkey, allow up to 500 g (1 lb) of uncooked turkey per person.

🌿 A 2 kg (4 lb) whole chicken will serve six people.

🌿 Allow approximately 250 g (8 oz) per person for whole chicken or bone-in chicken pieces – 500 g (1 lb) will serve two or three people.

🌿 For boneless, skinless chicken, allow approximately 125 g (4 oz) per person.

Food safety

🌿 Never allow raw poultry or poultry juices to come in contact with other food.

🌿 Use separate cutting boards and utensils for raw and cooked chicken. Wash them both thoroughly with hot soapy water after use.

🌿 To cut raw or roasted chicken into pieces, try poultry shears or sharp kitchen scissors.

🌿 Always ensure that poultry is cooked thoroughly. Undercooked poultry may contain bacteria that can cause food poisoning.

Freezing and thawing

🌿 Thaw frozen chicken in the refrigerator overnight – never on the kitchen bench or in the sink. Place the chicken in a large dish to catch any juices. (If you're in a hurry, you can speed up the process by leaving the bird in its wrapping and submerging it in cold water.)

🌿 For thawing, allow 10 hours per kg (5 hours per lb). Once thawed, use within 24 hours.

🌿 Never refreeze raw poultry that has already been frozen. However, you can freeze a cooked dish that contains previously frozen poultry.

🌿 Fresh poultry can be frozen for up to one year.

Chicken curry

Spicy but not fiery, this fragrant Malaysian-style curry is sure to be a much-loved dish. Serve with plenty of rice to soak up all the creamy coconut milk, and add some chopped fresh chilli if you like it hot.

SERVES 4 • PREP 15 MINUTES + 30 MINUTES MARINATING • COOK 45 MINUTES

5 cloves garlic, crushed

5 cm (2 inch) piece of fresh ginger,
   peeled and finely grated

2 red onions, finely chopped

2 tablespoons Malaysian curry powder
   (or use a medium curry powder)

1.5 kg (3 lb) chicken pieces

3 tablespoons vegetable oil

2 cups (500 ml/17 fl oz) coconut milk

500 g (1 lb) boiling (waxy) potatoes, peeled
   and cut into large chunks

4 spring onions (scallions), finely sliced

2 red chillies, finely sliced (optional)

steamed rice, to serve

1 Put the garlic, ginger and onions in a food processor with 2–3 tablespoons water. Process into a paste, then mix in the curry powder. Rub this paste all over the chicken pieces, then cover and allow to marinate in the refrigerator for 30 minutes.

2 Heat the oil in a large frying pan or wok over medium heat. Working in batches, add the chicken pieces with all of the marinade and brown on each side, taking care not to burn the paste. Add the coconut milk, scraping up all the spices from the bottom of the pan, and simmer for 15 minutes.

3 Add the potatoes and simmer for another 20 minutes, or until the potatoes are cooked and the sauce has thickened. Stir in the spring onions and garnish with the chilli, if using. Serve immediately, with steamed rice.

Tarragon chicken

This is a time-saving version of a French dish that traditionally uses a whole chicken, with tarragon butter inserted under the skin.

SERVES 4 · PREP 10 MINUTES · COOK 15 MINUTES

3 tablespoons unsalted butter
1 tablespoon olive oil
4 x 250 g (8 oz) boneless, skinless chicken breasts
2 spring onions (scallions), finely chopped
1 clove garlic, finely chopped
¼ cup (60 ml/2 fl oz) dry white wine
½ cup (125 ml/4 fl oz) pouring cream
1 tablespoon chopped fresh tarragon

1 Heat the butter and oil in a large frying pan over medium heat until the butter has melted. Add the chicken breasts and cook for 5 minutes, then turn and cook the other side for a further 5 minutes, or until the chicken is nicely browned and cooked through.

2 Add the spring onions and garlic and cook for 1 minute, or until the garlic has softened. Add the wine, cream and tarragon and cook for a further 2 minutes, stirring to coat the chicken.

3 Place the chicken breasts on warmed plates and spoon the sauce over the top. Serve with steamed vegetables.

So many herbs go wonderfully well with chicken. If you can't obtain tarragon, try fresh thyme or lemon thyme, chervil, dill or even basil in this dish. Rosemary and sage are good too, but use them sparingly so they don't overpower.

Seafood

Fish and shellfish require very little preparation and they positively benefit from a brief cooking time. They are extremely versatile too, so you can create a host of healthy and tempting dishes in next to no time.

Basics

Here are the best and simplest ways of preparing fish. Be careful not to overcook fish as the fragile flesh easily dries out. Fish is done when the flesh is opaque and flakes easily with a fork.

Barbecuing

Barbecuing is a tasty way to cook fish. Be sure to oil the barbecue plate so the fish doesn't stick. Cook whole oily fish like sardines, trout or mackerel for 4–8 minutes on each side, depending on the size. Marinate white fish if it is to be cooked straight on the barbecue, or wrap it in foil parcels with herbs and lemon juice. Cut chunky white fish into cubes and thread it onto skewers with vegetables for wonderful kebabs.

Braising

Fish is delicious braised with vegetables and a little fish stock or wine. Soften the chopped vegetables in a flameproof casserole dish first, then lay the fish on top and braise on the cooktop or in the oven. Allow 7–8 minutes for fillets and steaks, and about 20 minutes for a whole 1 kg (2 lb) fish.

'En papillote'

Cooking fish in parcels ensures the flesh stays moist. Stuff a whole fish with herbs or vegetables, wrap in foil and bake at 180°C (350°F/Gas 4). Allow about 10 minutes per 500 g (1 lb). Thick fillets or steaks can be parcelled in baking paper or foil with vegetables, herbs and a little wine or lemon juice.

Grilling

Oily fish such as herrings, mackerel and trout are great grilled (broiled) – their own healthy oils do all the basting! White fish should be marinated first so it doesn't dry out. Depending on its size and thickness, fish will take 4–12 minutes to cook.

Microwaving

Microwaving is an excellent way to cook fish: it retains all its moistness, natural flavour and nutrients, and takes only a few minutes. When microwaving fish pieces, add a little stock or lemon juice and cover with paper towel. When microwaving a whole fish, slash the skin a few times so it doesn't burst.

Pan-frying

Fish is delicious briefly pan-fried in a little oil or butter. If you use a non-stick frying pan or a ridged cast-iron chargrill pan and heat the pan well, you'll need only a tiny amount of fat. Pan-fried fish needs only 2–3 minutes cooking on each side, depending on the thickness of the fish.

Poaching

Poaching fish in milk, fish stock or water with a splash of wine brings out its flavour and keeps it very moist. The poaching liquid will retain the water-soluble vitamins from the fish, so keep it for a sauce or soup. Put a whole fish in a large pot with cold liquid to cover, put the lid on and bring to a gentle simmer (it should never boil). Poach for 8–12 minutes, then remove from the heat and leave to cool in the liquid.

Steaming

Steaming is one of the healthiest ways to cook fish as it uses no fat and, because the fish does not come into direct contact with liquid, most of the vital nutrients are retained. Steam the fish with herbs and aromatics to add flavour.

Hints and tips

Serving sizes

Allow 200 g (7 oz) per person when purchasing fish fillets. A whole fish of 2 kg (4 lb) will serve four people.

Buying fish

🦐 Fish and seafood is best eaten very fresh and in season. Ask at your local fish market for advice as varieties abound.

🦐 Choose fresh-smelling fish with glistening skin, bright eyes and firm flesh. Fish fillets should be moist and firm; shellfish should have a bright colour.

🦐 Frozen fish is a useful stand-by and retains its nutritional value. It is a particularly good choice when wild fish is out of season. (Farmed fish is available all year round.)

Storing fish

Store raw seafood in the refrigerator in a dish to catch any liquid and use within two days. Very fresh fish can be frozen for up to three months.

Crumbing fish

Preheat the oven to 200°C (400°F/Gas 6). In a bowl, mix together ¼ cup (30 g/1 oz) flour, 1 egg and 2 tablespoons milk, then stir in ¾ cup (30 g/1 oz) cornflake crumbs. Coat four 125 g (4 oz) boneless white fish fillets in the crumbs, place on a baking tray lined with baking paper and bake for 12–15 minutes.

Making a batter

In a bowl, mix together 1 cup (125 g/4 oz) flour, 1 teaspoon baking powder and ½ teaspoon salt. Slowly add ½ cup (125 ml/4 fl oz) milk and ½ cup (125 ml/4 fl oz) water and beat until smooth. Dip fish fillets into the batter, letting the excess drip off. Fry until golden brown.

A herb rub for seafood

In a small bowl mix together 2 tablespoons dried basil, 2 teaspoons dried thyme, 1 teaspoon dried sage and some salt and freshly ground black pepper. Coat fish or prawns (shrimp) with 1 tablespoon olive oil and sprinkle with the rub, pressing gently to help it stick. Cook in a lightly oiled pan.

Marinating fish

There are many marinades for fish. This one is fragrant and delicious. In a large ceramic dish, combine 2 teaspoons grated ginger, 4 crushed garlic cloves, 1 thinly sliced red onion, 1 chopped spring onion (scallion), 4 tablespoons soy sauce, 1 tablespoon sesame oil and some freshly ground black pepper. Add fish to the marinade and turn to coat. Cover and marinate in the refrigerator for no longer than 30 minutes.

Cooking shellfish

🦐 When cooking a live crustacean such as a lobster or crab, first wrap it in a damp tea towel (dish towel) and put it in the freezer for 1–2 hours to make it comatose. Then plunge it into a large saucepan of boiling water and quickly clamp on the lid. Cook crab for 10–12 minutes, whatever its size; lobsters need about 15 minutes for the first 500 g (1 lb) and then 10 minutes for each subsequent 500 g (1 lb).

🦐 Prawns (shrimp) can be poached, pan-fried, grilled (broiled), barbecued or stir-fried. Raw prawns take only a few minutes to change to a bright pink colour, which indicates they are done. If you are adding ready-cooked prawns to a dish, add them right near the end and cook them only very briefly so that they are just heated through.

🦐 Molluscs such as mussels and clams are usually steamed open, whereas oysters and scallops are more often prised open. Whether steamed, grilled, stir-fried or sautéed, cooking should be brief as overcooking will make the shellfish tough.

Salmon parcels

Cooking delicately textured fish such as salmon in foil or baking paper is an ideal way to retain all its taste and nutrients.

SERVES 4 · PREP 15 MINUTES · COOK 15 MINUTES

150 g (5 oz) baby English spinach leaves

4 x 200 g (7 oz) salmon fillets

2 limes, cut into 1 cm (½ inch) rounds

4 fresh makrut (kaffir lime) leaves, cut into slivers

1 large red chilli, finely sliced (optional)

½ cup (15 g/½ oz) fresh coriander (cilantro)

½ cup (15 g/½ oz) fresh Thai basil

2 spring onions (scallions), finely sliced

½ cup (125 ml/4 fl oz) coconut milk

1 tablespoon fish sauce

1 teaspoon sesame oil

½ cup (70 g/2½ oz) roughly chopped cashew nuts, toasted (optional)

1 Preheat the oven to 180°C (350°F/Gas 4). Lay four sheets of foil, each about 30 cm (12 inches) square, on a work surface. Divide the spinach among the foil squares and place a salmon fillet in the centre of each. Top each fillet with lime rounds, lime leaves, chilli (if using), coriander, Thai basil and spring onion.

2 In a small bowl, mix together the coconut milk, fish sauce and sesame oil.

3 Bring the four sides of each foil sheet up around the salmon fillets. Drizzle each fillet with 2 tablespoons of the coconut milk mixture, then wrap the foil securely around each fillet so the liquid doesn't leak out during baking.

4 Place the parcels on a baking tray and bake for about 12 minutes for medium–rare salmon, or until cooked to your liking. Serve the fish in the parcels, sprinkled with the cashew nuts if desired.

Thai basil has a warm, peppery taste and a lingering aniseed taste. Fennel fronds also have an aniseed taste and can be used instead.

Garlic prawns with potato chowder

Quickly sizzled in olive oil and still tasting of the sea, plump, juicy garlic prawns are hard to resist. Served on top of a thick, creamy chowder, they turn a simple meal into something special.

SERVES 4 · PREP 25 MINUTES · COOK 35 MINUTES

Potato chowder

2 tablespoons butter
1 large onion, finely chopped
4 cloves garlic, crushed
750 g (1½ lb) all-purpose potatoes,
    peeled and sliced
2 bay leaves
1 sprig fresh thyme
3 cups (750 ml/26 fl oz) chicken stock
150 ml (5 fl oz) pouring cream
salt and freshly ground black pepper
2 tablespoons chopped fresh chives

Garlic prawns

¼ cup (60 ml/2 fl oz) olive oil
12 large raw prawns (shrimp), peeled
    and deveined, tails left on
4 cloves garlic, crushed

1 To make the potato chowder, melt the butter in a large saucepan and gently sauté the onion and garlic for 3–5 minutes, or until softened. Add the potatoes, bay leaves, thyme sprig and stock. Bring to a boil, then reduce the heat and simmer for 20 minutes, or until the potatoes are soft. Remove and discard the bay leaves and thyme, then stir in the cream.

2 Allow the soup to cool a little, then blend to a smooth purée using a food processor or hand-held blender. Season to taste with salt and black pepper and reheat gently.

3 To make the garlic prawns, heat the olive oil in a frying pan over medium heat. Add the prawns and garlic and stir constantly until the prawns turn pink and curl up, taking care not to burn the garlic.

4 Ladle the soup into four warmed bowls and arrange three prawns in the centre of each. Sprinkle with the chives and serve.

Make a pile of garlic prawns and serve as a starter with crusty bread to soak up the garlicky oil and juices. Fry them with some chopped red chilli for extra kick, or sliced chorizo sausage for a smoky hit.

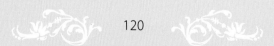

Vegetables and salads

Full of fabulous vitality, vegetables are ideal for all sorts of cooking methods: steaming, roasting, stewing, braising. They are perfect for barbecues, stir-fries and salads too, and their goodness always shines through.

Basics

Pick the freshest produce you can find, and buy your vegetables in season when they're at their very best. Buy locally whenever you can — you'll be doing what's best for the planet, your community and your tastebuds!

The best potatoes ever

Light mashed potatoes

Peel 1 kg (2 lb) floury potatoes (those with a high starch content, such as king edward, maris piper, russet or sebago). Cut them into large chunks, place in a saucepan and pour in enough boiling water to cover by 5 cm (2 inches). Bring to a boil, then reduce the heat and cook for 15–20 minutes, or until tender but not mushy. Drain well and return to the pan. Pour in ⅓–½ cup (100–125 ml/3–4 fl oz) hot milk and mash until smooth. Add 2 tablespoons olive oil or butter, season with salt and freshly ground black pepper, then beat with a wooden spoon until fluffy. Serve immediately. Serves 4–6.

Creamy mashed potatoes

Use desiree potatoes for the best result. Increase the butter to 80 g (2½ oz) and replace the milk with ¾ cup (200 g/7 oz) crème fraîche or sour cream.

Perfect roast potatoes

Preheat the oven to 220°C (425°F/Gas 7). Peel 1 kg (2 lb) of your favourite roasting potatoes (such as desiree, pontiac, bintje or new potatoes), then cut them into 5 cm (2 inch) chunks. Place in a large saucepan and pour in enough boiling water to cover. Cook for 5–6 minutes over medium heat, then drain the potatoes well and return them to the pan. Place a lid on the pan, give a good shake, then season well with salt. Heat 3 tablespoons olive oil in a roasting tin (baking pan), add the potatoes and transfer to the oven. Roast, turning occasionally, for 40–50 minutes, or until deliciously golden. Season with salt and serve immediately. Serves 4–6.

Ways to eat more vegetables

Serve them straight up Put a platter of sliced raw vegies – carrots, celery, cucumber, capsicum (bell pepper) – on the table each dinnertime and serve with a dip, salsa or vinaigrette. Or toss together a simple salad for a great way to start dinner.

Sizzle up a sauté Select two or three favourite vegetables and cut into bite-sized pieces. Heat a frying pan or small wok to a high temperature. Swirl a little olive oil in the pan until hot, then add the vegetables and toss until just cooked. Add seasonings such as salt, pepper, herbs, soy sauce or sesame oil, then simply toss again and serve.

Roast them Many vegetables develop a full-bodied, intense flavour when roasted. In winter, go for root vegetables such as parsnips, turnips, beetroots (beets) and potatoes. In summer, try mushrooms, zucchini (courgettes), tomatoes, capsicums (bell peppers) and onions. Cut into similar-sized chunks, toss in oil, vinegar and seasonings, place in a roasting tin (baking pan) and bake in a moderate oven for about 30 minutes.

Slurp them Just about any cooked (or leftover) vegetable can be puréed into a creamy, comforting soup.

Slip them into an omelette There are few vegetables that won't enhance an omelette, especially when a little grated or crumbled cheese is added!

Sneak them in everywhere Add chopped cooked spinach or grated carrot to the sauce you use to make lasagne. Increase the amount of vegetables and reduce the amount of meat you use in soups, stews and casseroles. To enhance the flavour and nutritional value of minced (ground) meat for burgers, meat loaves or bolognaise sauces, add up to a cup of your favourite grated or finely chopped raw vegetables to the mixture before shaping and cooking.

Hints and tips

Buying and storing vegetables

🌱 Buy vegetables as close to cooking time as possible, for optimum nutrient content, texture and flavour.

🌱 Store vegetables in the refrigerator, except for root vegetables such as potatoes, parsnips and onions, which keep best in a cool, dark and dry place.

🌱 Before cooking, wash vegetables thoroughly but quickly. Never soak them – water-soluble vitamins will be washed away.

Cooking vegetables

Barbecuing

Heat the barbecue plate to medium–high. Rub the vegetables with cooking oil or toss them in an oil-based marinade or vinaigrette before cooking. Use long-handled tongs to turn the vegetables once, halfway through the cooking time, or when they are lightly charred and almost tender.

Blanching

Vegetables are briefly cooked in a large amount of boiling water, then immersed in cold water to arrest the cooking process and to retain their bright colour.

Boiling

Hard vegetables such as green beans, broccoli and carrots are cooked in just enough rapidly boiling water to cover, and just long enough to freshen their colour and soften the texture. Bring water to the boil first, add the vegetables and cook uncovered or partially covered.

Braising

Vegetables are briefly sautéed in fat, then liquid is added to finish the cooking process. Braising works well with fibrous vegetables such as celery hearts, celeriac, leek and fennel. Root vegetables and leafy greens also become very tender.

Grilling (broiling)

The grill (broiler) should always be preheated first, and vegetables marinated or brushed with oil so they don't dry out in the intense dry heat, which browns the surface while cooking the inside. Fibrous vegetables such as celery and leeks are best if they are first blanched to soften them. Place the vegetables 10–15 cm (4–6 inches) from the heat source.

Microwaving

Microwaving is a fast, clean and convenient method for cooking many vegetables and retains their nutrients, crispness and colour. Place vegetables in a microwave-safe dish with a vented cover and add a small amount of water. The greater the volume of vegetables, the longer it will take for them to be cooked.

Sautéing

Cooking vegetables quickly in a small amount of fat over a relatively high heat, shaking the pan and stirring and tossing frequently to keep the food from sticking. Tender vegetables such as onion, zucchini (courgette) and mushrooms can be cut up and sautéed very quickly. Hard ones such as carrots, broccoli and cauliflower may benefit from a blanching to soften them slightly before sautéing.

Steaming

Cooking food on a rack above boiling or simmering liquid (usually water), covered beneath a lid. Cooking vegetables in the oven encased in baking paper or foil with a little liquid is also a form of steaming.

Stir-frying

Quickly cooking finely sliced vegetables in a wok or frying pan in a small amount of oil over high heat, stirring constantly. Vegetables should be cooked just until crisp-tender. Organised preparation is essential for successful stir-frying: chop and slice vegetables ahead of time and measure out all your seasonings.

Chargrilled vegetables

Put a dose of vitamins — and a rainbow splash of brightness — on your plate with this scrumptious mix of Mediterranean-style vegetables, enhanced with a balsamic glaze.

SERVES 4 • PREP 10 MINUTES • COOK 15 MINUTES

1 large red capsicum (bell pepper), seeds and
    membranes removed, then cut into strips
    2 cm (¾ inch) wide
1 zucchini (courgette), sliced
1 red onion, sliced
2 portobello mushrooms, stems removed and
    the caps cut into strips 2 cm (¾ inch) wide
2–3 tablespoons extra virgin olive oil
1 teaspoon dried oregano, crumbled
1 tablespoon balsamic vinegar
¼ teaspoon salt
¼ teaspoon freshly ground black pepper

1 Preheat the grill (broiler) or a chargrill pan or chargrill barbecue plate to medium–high.

2 Put the capsicum, zucchini, onion and mushrooms in a large bowl. Sprinkle with the olive oil and oregano and toss to coat. Spread the vegetables on the grill tray or chargrill in a single layer.

3 Grill (broil) or barbecue for 6–8 minutes, or until the vegetables are just becoming tender but are still a bit crisp and lightly flecked with brown. Turn them and cook for a further 5 minutes, or until done.

4 In a small bowl, mix together the vinegar, salt and black pepper. Arrange the vegetables on a platter and brush the vinegar mixture over them. Serve warm or at room temperature.

Cut vegetables for chargrilling into pieces that are not too thick and of uniform size so they'll cook quickly and evenly. To stop them drying out during the grilling process you can soak the pieces in cold water for 30 minutes first, then brush with olive oil before cooking.

Caesar salad

In 1924 in Tijuana, Mexico, Caesar Cardini caused a sensation when he first dished up a salad of lettuce, parmesan and croutons, dressed with garlic, lemon, egg, olive oil and worcestershire sauce. So can you!

SERVES 4 · PREP 30 MINUTES · COOKING 5 MINUTES

2 small heads of cos (romaine) lettuce
4 large leaves of iceberg lettuce
60 g (2 oz) chunk of parmesan
2 slices of sourdough bread, crusts removed
2 tablespoons olive oil

Anchovy dressing
4 anchovy fillets
1 clove garlic, roughly chopped
½ cup (125 ml/4 fl oz) olive oil
1 very fresh large egg yolk
2 tablespoons lemon juice
2 tablespoons dijon mustard
1 tablespoon worcestershire sauce
a pinch of sugar
salt and freshly ground black pepper

1 Cut the cos and iceberg lettuce leaves into bite-sized bits. Use a vegetable peeler or cheese grater to shave the parmesan into thin slivers.

2 To make the anchovy dressing, put the anchovy fillets and garlic in a bowl and mash to a paste. Whisk in the olive oil, egg yolk, lemon juice, mustard, worcestershire sauce and sugar. Season to taste with salt and black pepper.

3 To make the croutons, cut the bread into small cubes. Heat the olive oil in a large non-stick frying pan over medium heat. Add the bread cubes and cook until golden brown on all sides, taking care that they don't burn. Set aside and keep warm.

4 Arrange the lettuce and shaved parmesan on individual serving plates. Drizzle the dressing over the salad, scatter the croutons over the top and serve.

It's so easy to vary this classic salad. With the anchovy dressing you can simply use 1 cup (250 g/8 oz) good-quality mayonnaise instead of the olive oil and egg yolk. Or jazz it up by tossing in some cooked prawns (shrimp), cooked chicken tenderloins or lean chicken breast strips.

Desserts and baking

There's nothing more satisfying than a home-cooked sweet treat.
Something delightfully delicious to see you through those mid-morning
or mid-afternoon doldrums, and to round out the day.

Basics

The keys to successful baking are simple: always preheat the oven, have everything ready to go before you start mixing, measure the ingredients carefully, use the tin size suggested in the recipe – then straight into the oven. Superb!

Basic butter cake

Preheat the oven to 180°C (350°F/Gas 4). Grease a deep, 20 cm (8 inch) round cake tin and line the base with baking paper. Beat 185 g (6 oz) unsalted butter until very soft, using electric beaters. Add 1 cup (250 g/8 oz) caster (superfine) sugar and cream together until light and fluffy. Gradually beat in 3 large eggs, adding a teaspoon of self-raising flour with each addition to prevent curdling. Fold in another 2 cups (250 g/8 oz) flour, ¼ cup (60 ml/2 oz) milk, a few drops of vanilla extract and 1 teaspoon water. Spoon into the tin, smooth the surface and bake for 50–60 minutes, or until the cake is light golden and springs back when lightly pressed in the middle. Leave to cool in the tin for a few minutes, then turn out onto a wire rack to cool completely. Store in an airtight container for up to two days.

Chocolate brownies

Preheat the oven to 180°C (350°F/Gas 4). Line a 20 cm (8 inch) square cake tin with baking paper. Melt 125 g (4 oz) butter and 125 g (4 oz) dark chocolate in a small saucepan over very low heat. Remove from the heat and cool. Whisk 2 eggs in a bowl using electric beaters. Gradually add 1 cup (250 g/8 oz) caster (superfine) sugar, beating until the mixture is thick and foamy and leaves a ribbon-like trail when dribbled off the beaters. Mix in 1 teaspoon vanilla extract and the melted chocolate. Using a large spoon, fold ½ cup (60 g/2 oz) plain (all-purpose) flour and 1 cup (125 g/4 oz) chopped walnuts through. Pour into the tin and bake for 30 minutes, or until the top is a rich, deep brown, being watchful that it doesn't burn. Cool slightly in the tin, then cut into squares and turn out onto a wire rack to cool completely. Store in an airtight container for up to four days.

Meringues

Preheat the oven to 100°C (225°F/Gas ½) and line several large baking trays with baking paper. In a very clean, grease-free glass or stainless steel bowl, whisk 4 egg whites until very stiff, using an electric or balloon whisk. Measure out 1 cup (220 g/7 oz) caster (superfine) sugar and gradually add half the sugar, whisking well after each addition. Using a metal spoon or plastic spatula, lightly fold in the rest of the sugar. Immediately pipe or spoon the mixture onto the baking trays and bake for 2½–3 hours, or until firm and crisp but still white. Leave to cool completely on a wire rack, then carefully remove the baking paper. Store in an airtight container for up to three weeks.

Scones

Preheat the oven to 230°C (450°F/Gas 8) and lightly flour a baking tray. Sift 3 cups (450 g/14 oz) self-raising flour, a pinch of salt and ½ teaspoon baking powder into a bowl, then rub in 60 g (2 oz) butter until the mixture resembles breadcrumbs. Mix in 1 cup (250 ml/8 fl oz) milk using a round-bladed knife, adding a little extra milk if necessary to make a soft dough. Turn out onto a lightly floured surface and knead gently for a few seconds to bring the dough together. Roll out to 2 cm (¾ inch) thick, then stamp out as many rounds as possible using a 5 cm (2 inch) round pastry cutter. Gently re-knead and re-roll the trimmings and cut out more rounds, making about 12 in all. Place the scones, just touching one another, on the baking tray and brush the tops with milk. Bake for 10 minutes, or until the scones are well risen, golden and sound hollow when tapped on the base. Transfer to a wire rack to cool slightly. Serve warm with jam and cream; they are best eaten on the day of making.

Hints and tips

Baking basics

Common mixing methods

Creaming Beat room-temperature butter with sugar until the mixture is pale, light and fluffy, almost like whipped cream, then add beaten eggs and flour. This is the method for a sponge.

Melting Warm the butter with sugar until liquid, then mix in eggs and flour. This is used for gingerbread and some fruitcakes.

Rubbing in Rub cold, firm unsalted butter into flour with your fingertips until the mixture resembles crumbs, then mix in the sugar. Use this method for scones and pastries.

Whisking Whisk eggs with sugar until the mixture is thick enough to leave a 'ribbon' trail on the surface. This is the method for whisked sponges.

Testing for doneness

There are several ways to test if a cake or biscuit (cookie) is cooked. Whisked sponges should spring back when pressed lightly in the middle, whereas other cakes and some biscuits will be just firm or quite firm to the touch. In most cases, the exception being brownies, a skewer inserted into the centre should come out clean. Biscuits can scorch easily, so check them 5 minutes before the recommended baking time is up.

Freezing

Most cakes, scones, muffins and breads can be frozen without any deterioration in quality, but should be wrapped well to prevent moisture loss. To avoid damaging delicate cakes such as meringues and cheesecakes, freeze them unwrapped on a tray until firm, then wrap them and return to the freezer. Fillings, icings (frostings) or toppings made with cream, ricotta cheese, fromage frais or yogurt don't freeze well, so freeze a cake plain and fill or decorate it after thawing. Biscuits (cookies) freeze well and are very quick to thaw. Some biscuit doughs can be frozen raw, wrapped in plastic wrap or baking paper and overwrapped in foil. Then simply thaw the dough, slice and bake.

Quick and easy desserts

Fruit coulis

In a bowl, mash 250 g (8 oz) berries (such as raspberries, strawberries and blackberries) or soft fruit (such as kiwi fruit, peach, mango or papaya) using a fork. Mix in 1 tablespoon lemon juice and 1 tablespoon caster (superfine) sugar. (Alternatively, purée all the ingredients together in a food processor or blender.) Spoon the mixture into a fine sieve placed over a bowl and press the fruit through the sieve using a large spoon or spatula. Chill and serve with yogurt, crème fraîche or ice cream.

Mango fool

Purée the flesh from 2 very ripe mangoes (or other soft fruits such as banana or papaya) in a food processor or blender, then spoon into a glass serving bowl. Cover, chill and serve topped with 1 cup (250 g/8 oz) Greek-style yogurt and 4 tablespoons double (thick/heavy) cream.

Quick 'baked' apples

Core 2 apples, leaving the base intact. In a bowl, mix together 1 tablespoon soft brown sugar, 1½ teaspoons cinnamon, 1 teaspoon nutmeg and 1 tablespoon raisins. Spoon the mixture into the apples and dab 1 teaspoon butter on top of each. Place the apples in a deep microwave dish, cover and microwave for 3–4 minutes, or until tender.

Trifle

Cut slightly dry leftover cake into slices and drizzle with fruit juice (mixed with liqueur, if desired). Layer the cake slices in a bowl, alternating with layers of custard and berries or stewed fruit. Cover with plastic wrap and chill for at least 5 hours, or preferably overnight for the cake to soften and the flavours to develop. Cover with a thick layer of whipped cream and decorate with berries or slices of fresh fruit.

Peanut bites and almond cookies

These simple cookies require few ingredients and are quickly made.
They are just as quickly eaten!

SERVES 12–16 • PREP 20 MINUTES EACH • COOK 10–15 MINUTES

Peanut bites

1 cup (125 g/4½ oz) plain (all-purpose) flour
1 teaspoon baking powder
⅓ cup (70 g/2½ oz) soft brown sugar
70 g (2½ oz) butter
¼ cup (60 g/2 oz) crunchy peanut butter
1 egg
½ teaspoon ground mixed (pumpkin pie) spice
1 teaspoon grated orange zest

1 Preheat the oven to 190°C (375°F/Gas 5). Line a large baking tray with baking paper.

2 Sift the flour and baking powder into a large bowl. Add all the remaining ingredients and mix to a smooth dough using the dough hook of an electric mixer, or by hand.

3 Use two teaspoons to scoop 12 equal mounds of the mixture onto the baking tray, placing them about 2.5 cm (1 inch) apart.

4 Bake for 12–15 minutes, or until golden brown. Remove from the oven and leave on the baking tray for 2–3 minutes to cool a little and harden slightly. Transfer to a wire rack to cool completely.

Almond cookies

¼ cup (40 g/1½ oz) blanched almonds, finely chopped
1 egg
½ cup (110 g/4 oz) caster (superfine) sugar
½ teaspoon baking powder
½ cup (55 g/2 oz) ground almonds
1 cup (120 g/4 oz) semolina
½ teaspoon grated lemon zest
4 drops of almond extract

1 Preheat the oven to 200°C (400°F/Gas 6). Line a large baking tray with baking paper. Spread the almonds on a plate and set aside.

2 Crack the egg into a bowl, add the sugar and beat until pale and fluffy. Add the remaining ingredients and mix well.

3 With moistened hands, shape the dough into 16 walnut-sized balls. Dip one side of each ball into the almonds and place them on the baking tray 2 cm (¾ inch) apart, almond side up.

4 Bake for 8–10 minutes, or until well risen and golden. Leave to cool on the baking tray for 1 minute, then transfer to a wire rack to cool completely. Store in an airtight jar or tin. If desired, dust with a little icing (confectioner's) sugar just before serving.

Bay-scented panna cotta

Panna cotta is a wobbly Italian dessert that translates as 'cooked cream'. Instead of the vanilla, you could use a little ground cinnamon or cardamom.

SERVES 4 • PREP 20 MINUTES + 4 HOURS CHILLING • COOK 5 MINUTES

10 g (¼ oz) gelatine sheets
2 cups (500 ml/17 fl oz) milk
1 vanilla bean
2 fresh bay leaves, bruised
⅓ cup (70 g/2½ oz) caster (superfine) sugar
350 g (12 oz) crème fraîche
2 cups (400 g/13 oz) fresh berries
1 teaspoon sugar
2 teaspoons chopped fresh mint
juice of ½ lime

1 Soak the gelatine sheets in cold water for 2–3 minutes to soften.

2 Put the milk in a large saucepan. Split the vanilla bean lengthwise, scrape the seeds into the milk and add the vanilla pod with the bay leaves and caster sugar. Gently heat, stirring until the sugar dissolves. Add the gelatine leaves, stir to dissolve the gelatine, then remove from the heat and leave to cool slightly. Stir in the crème fraîche until well combined.

3 Remove the bay leaves and vanilla, then pour the mixture into four lightly oiled 150 ml (5 fl oz) moulds. Refrigerate for at least 4 hours, or until set.

4 In a bowl, toss the berries with the sugar, mint and lime juice and leave to stand for 5 minutes.

5 To unmould the panna cotta, carefully slide a thin knife around the inside of the moulds, then invert onto serving plates. Serve with the berries.

Turning desserts out of moulds can be tricky. For a successful result, always lightly coat the moulds with an oil such as peanut or almond oil. Dip the moulds very briefly into a bowl of hot water to loosen the desserts, then carefully invert onto serving plates.

149

DESSERTS AND BAKING

 149

Jams, preserves and sauces

No commercial product can capture the heartwarming essence of homemade jams and sauces. Stock your pantry with juicy jams and preserves, and make your own sauces for pasta, vegetables and meat dishes.

Basics

Down the ages canny cooks have found ways to capture produce in its prime to relish throughout the year. They also knew how the simplest fare could be enhanced with a naturally luscious sauce!

Béchamel sauce

Melt 60 g (2 oz) butter in a saucepan over medium–high heat until it foams. Add ⅓ cup (50 g/1½ oz) plain (all-purpose) flour and stir for 1–2 minutes, or until the mixture is bubbling and no lumps remain. Remove from the heat and gradually whisk in 4 cups (1 litre/35 fl oz) milk until smooth. Return to the heat and stir for 10–12 minutes, or until the sauce thickens and coats the back of the spoon. Remove from the heat, stir in ¼ teaspoon salt, a pinch of nutmeg, and some grated parmesan if desired.

Tomato sauce

Heat 1 tablespoon olive oil in a large saucepan over medium heat. Sauté 1 crushed garlic clove and 1 chopped onion for 3–4 minutes, or until soft but not browned. Add 1 tablespoon tomato paste (concentrated purée) and stir constantly for 1 minute. Add 800 g (28 oz) canned chopped tomatoes, reduce the heat and simmer for 10 minutes, or until thickened. Stir in 1 teaspoon sugar, ½ cup (30 g/1 oz) chopped fresh basil and 4 tablespoons chopped fresh flat-leaf parsley and season to taste. Add minced (ground) beef for bolognaise sauce.

Apple sauce

Peel, core and roughly chop 500 g (1 lb) apples. Place in a saucepan with 2 tablespoons cold water and cook over low heat for 10 minutes, or until soft. Mash with a vegetable masher, or for a smoother sauce, purée in a blender or food processor. Stir in 1½ tablespoons butter and sweeten to taste with caster (superfine) sugar if desired. Depending on how sweet you make it, this sauce can be served with sweet or savoury dishes.

Mint sauce

Put ¾ cup (30 g/1 oz) chopped fresh mint and 2 tablespoons caster (superfine) sugar in a bowl. Add ¼ cup (60 ml/2 fl oz) boiling water and stir until the sugar dissolves. Stir in ½ cup (125 ml/4 fl oz) white wine vinegar or malt vinegar and serve.

Citrus marmalade

Wash 1 kg (2 lb) oranges and 2 lemons. Cut in half and squeeze the juice into a preserving pan or large stainless steel pan. Tie the seeds and membranes in a muslin (cheesecloth) bag. Thinly shred the peels and add to the pan with the bag and 9 cups (2.25 litres/ 80 fl oz) water. Bring to a boil, then simmer gently, uncovered, for 2 hours, or until reduced by half – the peel should be very tender. Remove the bag and squeeze any liquid back into the pan. Add 8 cups (1.75 kg/3½ lb) sugar and stir over very low heat until completely dissolved. Bring to a boil and boil rapidly for 15 minutes, or until setting point is reached (105°C/221°F on a sugar thermometer). Remove from the heat, skim off any froth and cool for 5 minutes, or until a thin skin forms. Stir gently to distribute the peel. Ladle into warm, sterilised jars, cover and seal.

Strawberry jam

Hull 2 kg (4 lb) firm strawberries and place in a preserving pan or large stainless steel pan with the juice of 1 lemon. Heat gently until the juices start to run, then mash to the desired texture. Cook to a thick slush, stirring often. Add 9 cups (2 kg/4 lb) sugar and stir over low heat until completely dissolved. Bring to a boil and boil steadily for 8 minutes, stirring frequently, until setting point is reached. Ladle into warm, sterilised jars, cover and seal.

Rhubarb and vanilla jam

This jam is a rhubarb lover's delight – spread it thickly on fresh bread or toast, or enjoy with scones and cream

Makes 2 jars

Ready in 45 minutes, plus cooling

Price per tablespoon 20p

700g **rhubarb** (trimmed weight), cut into 2cm pieces

700g **jam sugar** (with pectin added – see Chef's Tip)

1 **vanilla pod**, cut in half lengthways

Juice of 1 **orange**

1 Preheat the oven to 140C/120C Fan/Gas 1. Wash two or three jam jars in hot, soapy water, then rinse and put in a warm oven to dry, or wash on a hot dishwasher cycle, then keep warm. Put two plates in the freezer ready to test for setting.

2 Put the rhubarb, sugar, vanilla and orange juice in a large, wide-based pan and heat gently, stirring occasionally, until the sugar has dissolved.

3 Increase the heat and bring to the boil. Boil rapidly for 10 minutes, then test for setting. To do this, put a teaspoon of jam on one of the chilled plates, then push it gently with your finger. If the surface wrinkles, the jam is ready. If not, boil again for 2 minutes, then retest. Repeat until it's ready.

4 Skim any scum off the surface and remove the vanilla pod. Leave the jam for 15 minutes, then pour into the jars. Cover with jam pot covers, following the instructions on the pack.

Rhubarb crumble flan

The pastry case adds an extra dimension to this classic family favourite

Serves 6

Ready in 1 hour

Price per serving £1.02

- 400g **rhubarb** (trimmed weight), cut into 2cm pieces
- 75g **caster sugar**
- 300g **ready-to-roll shortcrust pastry**
- 100g **plain flour**, plus extra for rolling out
- 1 level tsp **ground cinnamon**
- 50g **butter**, plus extra for greasing
- 100g **demerara sugar**
- 75g **almonds**, roughly chopped
- 50g **ground almonds**
- 3tbsp **apricot jam or shredless orange marmalade**

1. **Preheat the oven** to 200C/ 180C Fan/Gas 6. Put the rhubarb in a single layer in a shallow greased dish and sprinkle on the caster sugar. Cover with foil and cook in the oven for 15 minutes. Remove the foil, turn the pieces over and cook, uncovered, for another 10 minutes or until tender. Set aside.

2. **Meanwhile, roll out** the pastry on a lightly floured surface and use to line a 23cm flan tin. Prick the base. Lay a piece of foil inside and weight it down with baking beans or rice. Bake for 10 minutes, then remove the foil and beans or rice and bake for another 5 minutes. Reduce the oven temperature to 190C/ 170C Fan/Gas 5.

3. **Sift the flour** and cinnamon into a bowl. Add the butter and rub in. Stir in the demerara sugar and both types of almonds.

4. **Spread the jam** or marmalade in the base of the flan case. Drain the juice off the rhubarb and put the rhubarb in the flan case. Sprinkle the crumble on top.

5. **Bake for another** 20 minutes. Serve warm with cream or custard.

No-Fail Orange Curd Recipe aka Homemade Orange Curd

When oranges are in season you must make homemade orange curd. This simple, easy and effortless recipe for no-fail orange curd is the best you will ever taste. Sweet, tangy with a melt in the mouth luxurious texture. An orange curd that takes no more than 20 minutes to prepare and can be used as a filling for cakes, pies, and desserts is a must-have recipe on hand.

4.87 from 30 votes

Course: Breakfast, Dessert   Cuisine: French   Keyword: Orange Curd Recipe
Prep Time: 10 minutes   Cook Time: 10 minutes   Total Time: 20 minutes
Servings: 2 cups   Calories: 761kcal   Author: Veena Azmanov   Cost: $5

Equipment

- Double Boiler
- Mixing Bowl
- Saucepan (1.5 quarts)
- Sieve
- Spatula

Ingredients

- 3 Egg yolks (large)
- 1 Whole egg (large)
- 2 tbsp Cornstarch
- 1/2 tbsp Orange zest
- 1/2 tbsp Lemon zest
- 180 ml Orange juice
- 4 tbsp Lemon juice
- 100 grams Sugar fine grain
- 113 grams Unsalted butter chilled, cubed
- 1/4 tsp Salt

Instructions

Prepare

1. Measure all ingredients before you start.

2. Cut the butter into cubes - keep chilled.

3. Place oranges and lemon in the microwave for 10 seconds before you cut and squeeze this will make it easy.

4. Warm the orange juice for about 30 secs.

Cook curd over a double boiler or a saucepan and bowl (read more above)

1. In the top bowl of a double boiler- before you place it on the hot water

2. Add egg and yolks, sugar, salt, cornstarch, and zests.

3. Whisk until light and fluffy - sugar should almost melt.

4. Add orange juice and lemon juice slowly into the egg mixture.

5. Now place the bowl on the double boiler/hot water pot.

6. Continue to stir on low. The mixture should cook with just the steam from the water in the saucepan below.

7. About 8 to 10 minutes - you will notice the foam that was caused by whipping the egg mixture will slowly disappear and the mixture will start to thicken.

8. Continue to stir until it coats the back of your wooden spoon or spatula.

9. Remove from heat.

10. Gradually add cubes of butter one at a time. Make sure each piece is well incorporated.

11. The mixture will continue to thicken as it cools.

12. Once all the butter has been incorporated, strain it through a mesh or a strainer to remove the zest. This will also give you a smooth creamy curd.

Notes

Storage

- The curd is best stored in a mason or glass jar in the fridge. The presence of eggs in lemon or orange curd makes it a perishable filling so any item that has homemade lemon or orange curds such as cakes and pie need to be placed in the fridge.
- Avoid keeping fruit curd or citrus fillings in metal containers as it can react with the metal.

- Egg yolks can react with the metal such as aluminum and cause it to become green in color

Nutrition

Calories: 761kcal | Carbohydrates: 62g | Protein: 8g | Fat: 55g | Saturated Fat: 32g | Cholesterol: 496mg | Sodium: 449mg | Potassium: 180mg | Fiber: 0g | Sugar: 54g | Vitamin A: 2010IU | Vitamin C: 38.1mg | Calcium: 61mg | Iron: 1.1mg

Recipe by Veena Azmanov

NO-FAIL ORANGE CURD RECIPE - HOMEMADE ORANGE CURD

When oranges are in season you must make homemade orange curd. This simple, easy and effortless recipe for no-fail orange curd is the best you will ever taste. Sweet, tangy with a melt in the mouth luxurious texture. An orange curd that takes no more than 20 minutes to prepare and can be used as a filling for cakes, pies, and desserts is a must-have recipe on hand.

Orange curd with fresh oranges is a must-have. I mean must-have. The sweet oranges in a custard-like filling are out of this world. Personally, I love to add some lemon in there to give it a little zing from my lemon curd. By now you must have tried my lemon curd or at least seen my lemon curd video. It's simple, easy and really luxurious. It's a no-fail method because I cook it low and slow. As a result, you will never have a curdled curd whether you make lemon or orange curd.

DOUBLE BOILER, SAUCEPAN & BOWL FOR OUR ORANGE CURD RECIPE

The common equipment used to make curds or melt chocolate is called double boiler or Baine Maire - Which basically means two pots - that sit comfortably within each other as below. You can do this at home - just find a sauce panand a mixing bowl that sit comfortably so the bottom is just tad bigger than the top.

INGREDIENTS AND SUBSTITUTES (SAVE/PIN)

- **Oranges** - Use the measure of orange juice not the number of oranges when making this recipe. So if a recipe says 1/2 cup juice (3 to 4 oranges) usually the number is a guide - the actual measurement you want to use is 1/2 cup or 60 ml. This can make a big difference.

- **Lemon** - A little tart taste in contrast to the sweet seasonal oranges works a treat. Unless of course, you have sour oranges than lemons won't do justice. Instead, I suggest you add all orange juice.

- **Caster Sugar** - Caster sugar is usually a fine grain sugar. Use a fine grain sugar that will dissolve easily in the eggs. If you don't find caster sugar just pulse the regular sugar in a food processor and that will help give you a smooth finish. The amount of sugar used here presumes you have beautiful sweet seasonal oranges. If, however, the oranges are not sweet I highly recommend you add a few tbsp more of sugar. And yet, NO more than 1/4 cup or 30 grams though.

- Egg yolks - The color of yolks will determine the end color of your orange curd. So if you use light yolks you will have pale yellow color curd. A bright golden yellow or orange is much preferred. I'm using free-range eggs that have a nice orange color today.

- **Artificial colors** - I never use any artificial coloring in my lemon curd, but often I use orange curd in my cakes as filling. So sometimes I do add a dab of orange color just so it will be obvious on the cake. Orange color layers look nicer between two vanilla or chocolate layers.

CAN I MAKE THIS A SUGAR-FREE ORANGE CURD?

Yes, you can. Just replace the 1/2 cup sugar with either 1 tbsp stevia or similar.
If you prefer, you can also substitute sugar with 1/4 cup honey, or 1/3 cup agave syrup

USEFUL TIPS AND TOOLS:

- You will need a large saucepan with a bowl that can fit over it to create a homemade double boiler or

- You can also buy a double boiler that works best to melt chocolate, prepare pastry cream or curds.

- A whisk works best to ensure you have a smooth curd.

- Remove from heat.

- Gradually add cubes of butter one at a time. Make sure each piece is well incorporated.

- The mixture will continue to thicken as it cools.

- Once all the butter has been incorporated, strain it through a mesh or a strainer to remove the zest. This will also give you a smooth creamy curd.

STORAGE

- The curd is best stored in a mason or glass jar in the fridge. The presence of eggs in lemon or orange curd makes it a perishable filling. So any item that has homemade lemon or orange curds such as cakes and pie needs to be placed in the fridge.

- Avoid keeping fruit curd o

- citrus fillings in metal containers as it can react with the metal.

- Egg yolks can react with the metal such as aluminum and cause it to become green in color.

TIP AND TROUBLESHOOTING

- Juice the oranges easily - a great way to exact as much juice from oranges is to microwave the fruits for a few seconds (10 seconds).

- Warm the orange juice - warming the juice helps it incorporate into the egg yolks well.

- Egg yolks / Whole eggs - I find that all egg yolks have a higher risk of curdling but the one whole egg does help stabilize it.

- Use a spatula to gauge the thickness of the curd.

- Straining the curd thru a fine mesh or sieve will give you a smooth velvet-like curd by removing any curdles eggs

- A mason jar works best to store the curd once it's ready

HOW TO MAKE NO-FAIL ORANGE CURD (SAVE/PIN)

PREPARE

- Measure all ingredients before you start.

- Cut the butter into cubes - keep chilled.

- Place oranges and lemon in the microwave for 10 seconds before you cut and squeeze this will make it easy.

- Warm the orange juice for about 30 secs.

COOK CURD

- In the top bowl of a double boiler- before you place it on the hot water

  - Add egg and yolks, sugar, salt, cornstarch, and zests.

  - Whisk until light and fluffy - sugar should almost melt.

  - Add orange juice and lemon juice slowly into the egg mixture.

  - Now place the bowl on the double boiler/hot water pot.

  - Continue to stir on low. The mixture should cook with just the steam from the water in the saucepan below.

  - About 8 to 10 minutes - you will notice the foam that was caused by whipping the egg mixture will slowly disappear and the mixture will start to thicken.

  - Continue to stir until it coats the back of your wooden spoon or spatula.

- Whip eggs and sugar until light and fluffy - If you whip the eggs with sugar until the sugar almost dissolves it prevents the egg from curdling.

- Do not let the curd boil - cooking on low will prevent the curd from curdling. If the curd boils, it will give you a lemon-flavored scrambled eggs. So no matter how boring - cook on low heat for 10 to 15 mins.

- If you find the curd steaming up - take it off the heat for a few seconds this will help stabilize it.

- How to know if the curd is done? You can use a thermometer and check until the curd reaches 170 F., But I find the best test is taste. Once the curd is thick and coats the back of a wooden spoon, taste it. It should not have any taste of eggs or cornstarch. If necessary cook for 30 secs more.

Add butter slowly - this will help bring the temperature of the curd down slowly without curdling.

How long will this orange curd last?

If sealed and properly stored orange curd and be kept in the fridge for three months, however, once you have opened the jar do not keep the open jar for more than ten days to a maximum of 2 weeks. The curd on the surface will get slightly darker when exposed to air, but it is not a health concern.

Can I freeze orange curd?

Yes, lemon curd freezes well and can be kept for up to 1 year if stored properly. For best results, thaw in the refrigerator overnight or 24 hours before use.

-

Hints and tips

Before you start

When making jams and preserves, buy good-quality fruit or vegetables that are free of blemishes or bruises, as second-grade produce won't set as well or taste as good. Also make sure your produce is not under-ripe or over-ripe.

Preparing jam jars

Warm your jars in an oven preheated to 140°C (275°F/Gas 1) for about 5 minutes, to ensure that the glass does not crack when you pour in the hot jam. Oven warming also helps to ensure that freshly washed jars are absolutely dry, which helps keep them free from bacterial contamination.

Peeling and paring for marmalade

Choose ripe citrus with smooth skin – preferably fruit that has not been waxed. Scrub and dry the fruit. For fine-shred marmalade, pare off the zest and slice it into very thin strips. For thin-cut and coarse-cut marmalade, cut off and discard the ends, stand the fruit upright and cut away the peel, avoiding the inner white pith. Now cut each strip of peel into thin strips for thin marmalade, or short thick strips for coarse-cut. Chop the flesh up roughly, reserving the juice, pith and seeds. (You can speed up the job by chopping unpeeled oranges straight into a food processor, but the processed peel will be chunky and uneven.) Use as recipe directs.

Cooking jam

When making a jam or preserve, always use a large pan so it boils freely, and be sure to stir frequently with a wooden spoon.

Once all the sugar has dissolved and the jam is boiling rapidly, it will start to look like jam in about 10 minutes. Test it as soon as you think it is ready as you must not overboil the jam, which could make it dark and ruin the flavour.

Testing the setting point for jam

The acid, pectin and sugar levels must all be in the right proportions for jam to become firm.

The most accurate method for testing is to stir the jam and then insert a sugar thermometer. Do not let the thermometer touch the bottom or sides of the pan, and keep testing while the jam boils. A proper set should be obtained when the temperature of the jam reaches 105°C (221°F).

If you don't have a sugar thermometer, remove the pan from the heat to prevent the contents overcooking, put a small quantity of jam onto a pre-chilled plate and place it in the refrigerator to rest for a few minutes. As soon as the jam is cold enough, push a finger gently through it. If the surface of the jam shows wrinkles, setting point has been reached.

Clear jam or jelly will fall from a spoon in a wavy curtain, not a stream, when it is ready.

Sealing jars

The best way to seal a jar for long storage is to fill it with hot jam and cover it immediately, using a screw-top or spring-clamp lid.

If the jam is being stored in a cool, dry, well-ventilated place, you can use sealing lids instead. Put a disc of waxed paper, waxed side down, on the surface of the jam and smooth it over with your finger to remove any air pockets. Then cover the jar with a cellophane circle made moist by wiping with a damp cloth. Place the cellophane round over the jar lid, damp side up, and secure it with a rubber band.

Storing jams and preserves

Allow the sealed, sterilised jars to cool completely, then label each one, indicating their contents and the date of making. Store in a cool, dark place and use within one year. Once opened, store in the refrigerator and use within one month.

Herb and spice pickles

Many pickles rely on spices for their assertive taste. The fresher the spice, the better the result, so it's best to buy little and often.

SERVES 12–16 • PREP 25 MINUTES EACH • COOK 15 MINUTES EACH

Chilli jam

1½ cups (250 g/8 oz) bottled chargrilled
   capsicums (bell peppers), chopped
2 long red chillies, roughly chopped
1 small red chilli, roughly chopped
¼ cup (60 ml/2 fl oz) olive oil
1 small brown onion, finely chopped
2 cloves garlic, finely chopped
1 tablespoon grated palm sugar (jaggery)
   or dark brown sugar
1 tablespoon fish sauce
2 teaspoons tamarind paste
1 tablespoon finely chopped fresh coriander
   (cilantro)
1 tablespoon finely chopped fresh mint

1 Put the capsicums and chillies in a food processor and blend until smooth.

2 Heat the olive oil in a small saucepan. Add the onion and sauté over medium heat for 2 minutes, or until softened. Add the garlic and cook for 30 seconds.

3 Add the capsicum mixture, sugar, fish sauce and tamarind paste and cook for 10 minutes over low heat, stirring occasionally. Remove from the heat, stir in the herbs and bottle until needed. Serve with barbecued foods.

Spicy eggplant relish

2 tablespoons vegetable oil
1 large red chilli, finely chopped
1 clove garlic, finely chopped
1 tablespoon finely grated fresh ginger
1 teaspoon ground turmeric
1 teaspoon mustard seeds
1 eggplant (aubergine), cut into 1 cm
   (½ inch) cubes
1 teaspoon salt
¼ cup (60 ml/2 fl oz) white wine vinegar
1 tablespoon sugar
3 tablespoons roughly chopped fresh
   coriander (cilantro)

1 Heat the vegetable oil in a saucepan over medium heat. Add the chilli, garlic, ginger, turmeric and mustard seeds and cook for 1 minute, or until fragrant, stirring often.

2 Add the eggplant, salt, vinegar, sugar and ½ cup (125 ml/4 fl oz) water. Cook for 10–12 minutes over low heat, stirring occasionally and adding a little extra water if the mixture becomes dry.

3 Remove from the heat, stir the coriander through and bottle until needed. Serve with eggs, chicken or fish.

Classic mayonnaise

This mayonnaise is perfect for potato salads and pasta salads, and is a basis for other creamy sauces. Spices or herbs can be added to the recipe as desired.

SERVES 12 · PREP 5 MINUTES

2 very fresh egg yolks
1 teaspoon dijon mustard
2 tablespoons white wine vinegar or lemon juice
1 cup (250 ml/8 fl oz) olive oil
salt and freshly ground white pepper

1 In a bowl, whisk together the egg yolks, mustard and vinegar.

2 Using an electric whisk, gradually add the olive oil – first drop by drop, then in a slow, steady stream. (If the mixture curdles or splits, add a little hot water and beat vigorously until it comes together.)

3 Season to taste with salt and white pepper, then cover and store in the refrigerator. Use within a few days.

To make a seafood cocktail sauce, add 4 tablespoons tomato sauce (ketchup), 1 teaspoon worcestershire sauce and a few drops of Tabasco. For tartare sauce, add 1 tablespoon finely chopped pickled cucumbers, 3 teaspoons chopped capers, 3 teaspoons chopped fresh flat-leaf parsley and 3 teaspoons chopped onion or chives.

JAMS, PRESERVES AND SAUCES

165

JAMS, PRESERVES AND SAUCES

Kitchen notes

Whatever recipe you cook from, the following tips and hints will help you to get the best from your ingredients and make the most of your kitchen.

Stocking the pantry

Keep your pantry well stocked with the basics and you will always have the makings of a healthy and satisfying meal, even when you don't have time to shop.

Dry ingredients

Flour (plain/all-purpose and self-raising) Cornflour (cornstarch) Sugar (granulated/white, caster/superfine and soft brown) Rice (basmati, long-grain, or jasmine and risotto) Pasta (various shapes) Noodles (including wok-ready/pre-cooked and instant) Couscous Rolled oats Red lentils Nuts Seeds Dried fruit Stock cubes and/or powder in various flavours Salt and black pepper Herbs and spices

Bottles and jars

Oils (olive, for drizzling over salads, and vegetable oil, for frying) Vinegar (red wine or white wine, balsamic) Soy sauce Worcestershire sauce Roasted capsicums (bell peppers) in oil Artichoke hearts in oil Sun-dried tomatoes in oil (or in vacuum packs) Tomato paste (concentrated purée) Passata (puréed tomatoes) Pesto Curry paste Tomato sauce Mayonnaise Olives Chutney Mustard (dijon and/or wholegrain) Preserves, spreads and syrups (jam, marmalade, peanut butter, golden syrup, maple syrup) Coconut milk and cream Sherry, brandy and rum

Cans

Chopped and whole tomatoes Baked beans Corn Chickpeas Various beans, such as red kidney and cannellini French-style green (puy) lentils Tuna, salmon and other fish Canned fruit in juice

Keeping bugs at bay

Dry ingredients such as flour, pasta and grains are subject to weevil infestation. There are a few ways to prevent this. Freezing just-bought, unopened packets for 48 hours will kill any eggs already in the foods. Afterwards, store dry ingredients in sealed plastic containers or glass jars to prevent infestation; weevils can easily chew through plastic packets. If you do notice moths in your food cupboards or weevils in packets of food, clean out the cupboards and discard all foods containing weevils or traces of them, such as cobwebs or small holes in the packaging. Freeze any other food packages for 48 hours as above.

Storing foods

Correct storage extends the life of foods and prevents the growth of harmful organisms that may cause illness.

Tips for safe storage

Put fresh meats straight into the refrigerator as soon as you return from shopping. Keep them in their sealed packs or put unpacked meat on a plate and wrap in plastic wrap (cling film). Make sure that raw meats are kept away from cooked food. Sliced cooked meats, such as ham and salami, must be stored away from raw meats. Once opened, place bacon and cooked meats in a sealed container and use within a few days.

Always refrigerate cooked food on a shelf above raw food to avoid the possibility of raw juices dripping onto it and contaminating it. Make sure that raw food is in a dish or container that will prevent leakage.

Unless you are going to use it within an hour, store strongly flavoured food (such as some cheeses) in plastic containers so the smell doesn't taint other foods.

Cover or tightly wrap any items that have been opened, and keep lids on jars and tops or corks on bottles. Arrange them so that their labels can be easily seen, which will prompt you to use them and not forget they are there.

Cans rust in the fridge, so transfer food from opened cans to sealed plastic containers before putting them into the fridge. Sauces in jars and tubes (such as mayonnaise, pesto, curry paste, horseradish, tomato paste and garlic paste) can be stored in the pantry until they are opened, but then need to be kept refrigerated and used before their use-by date.

Remember that use-by dates apply only when a product is sealed. Once opened, most packs of food should be used within two or three days.

Never put hot or warm food in the refrigerator, as it will raise the temperature. Allow cooked food to cool completely first.

If your refrigerator doesn't have one, invest in a fridge thermometer so you can see if the temperature goes outside the recommended range of 0–5°C (32–41°F).

Tips for safe freezing

Always cool then chill foods before you freeze them.

Freeze food quickly, but thaw it slowly, preferably in the fridge.

Never refreeze anything that has been frozen and thawed or is past its best. However, raw food that has been frozen and then cooked can be frozen again.

Wrap foods well or put them in sealed containers – freezer bags, ice cream or yogurt tubs and foil dishes – so they don't get freezer burn (caused by the icy air drying the food).

Freeze food in sensible portion sizes. Spread chicken and fish fillets out on a baking tray and open freeze, then transfer the individual portions to a freezer bag, squeeze out the air and seal. You can then take out just how much you need.

Label containers with the content and date of freezing, and arrange the oldest food towards the front of the freezer.

Try to use foods within two to three months of freezing.

When buying meat or fish to freeze, check that it has not already been frozen.

How long does fresh food keep?

Most items you buy from a supermarket for storage in the refrigerator will have a use-by date. If foods are fresh or not labelled, here are some general guidelines.

Raw food

Two days fish; **two to three days** green vegetables, salad and soft fruits; **three days** meat, sausages and poultry; **up to one week** cheese, eggs and milk; **one week** bacon.

Cooked food

One day cooked rice; **one to two days** cooked vegetables and cooked pasta or grains; **two to three days** casseroles, curries and stews; **one week** deli meats and fish. **Leftovers** can be covered and kept in the refrigerator for a day or two.

In the refrigerator or not?

Some foods should be stored at room temperature: tomatoes, to develop their flavour; avocados, to ripen properly; onions, potatoes and root vegetables (best stored in a vegetable rack in a cool, preferably dark, place); and most fruit, except berries. Bananas will go black if refrigerated.

In the refrigerator

Milk ❦ Butter ❦ Cheese ❦ Eggs ❦ Fruit juice ❦ Raw meat and fish ❦ Cooked meat and fish ❦ Bacon ❦ Yogurt ❦ Carrots ❦ Celery ❦ Leeks ❦ Seasonal greens ❦ Stir-fry vegetables ❦ Capsicums (bell peppers) ❦ Mushrooms (keep them in a paper bag, not plastic, so they don't sweat) ❦ Salad leaves ❦ Beans ❦ Zucchini (courgettes) ❦ Cucumber ❦ Radishes ❦ Spring onions (scallions) ❦ Berries ❦ Fresh herbs ❦ Grapes

Out of the refrigerator

Avocados ❦ Garlic ❦ Onions ❦ Potatoes ❦ Pumpkin (winter squash) ❦ Red onions ❦ Sweet potatoes ❦ Tomatoes ❦ Apples ❦ Bananas ❦ Kiwifruit ❦ Lemons ❦ Mandarins ❦ Mangoes ❦ Oranges ❦ Pears ❦ Stone fruit

Kitchen thrift

If you have an unexpected guest, or not quite enough of a key ingredient, here are some ideas to make things go further.

❦ To make a small roasting chicken feed more people, joint the chicken and use the pieces to make a casserole or curry and serve with rice and a side dish.

❦ If you're short of potatoes, try mashing them with an equal quantity of carrots or pumpkin or sweet potato for a colourful, healthy mash. Alternatively, roast the potatoes with other root vegetables such as carrots and parsnips.

❦ If you don't have enough fish to go round, cut it into pieces and use in a chunky one-pot meal. Alternatively, poach the fish and combine with mashed potato to make fishcakes.

❦ Make desserts go further or make it look as though a small portion was intentional. Serve an elegant sliver of tart with a dollop of cream or crème fraîche and dust with icing (confectioners') sugar, or scoop a modest portion of ice cream into an elegant stemmed glass and drizzle with fruit coulis or chocolate sauce.

❦ Dress up a plain cake and make it bigger by cutting it into layers, spreading with cream and piling on fruit.

Something from nothing

Transform leftovers into new meals. Store any remains in a sealed container in the refrigerator and use them up the next day or in two days at the most.

Cooked rice Toss leftover rice with chopped raw vegetables and dressing to make a salad, or stir-fry it with vegetables and a little meat to make fried rice.

Cooked pasta If there's enough pasta left over for another serving, stir it into a pasta sauce, add some cooked vegetables and perhaps some chopped ham, then spoon into individual dishes, sprinkle with grated cheese and bake until golden. Alternatively, add it to a minestrone-style soup.

Cooked meat or poultry Leftovers from a roast can be added to almost anything: sandwiches, salads, sauces, fillings for pies or pancake parcels, omelettes, hashes and rice and pasta dishes. For instance, if you have leftover roast chicken, use it in a pie, frittata or risotto. Scraps are also great combined with mashed potato and shaped into croquettes or patties and fried.

Cooked fish and shellfish Small amounts of fish and shellfish are very versatile and can be added to salads, sauces, soups, stir-fries, risottos or pizza toppings, or used in fishcakes, tarts and pastry parcels. You can also use leftover cooked fish in a frittata or to make croquettes or patties.

Cooked vegetables Add to soups. Use as fillings for an omelette, or add them to a tortilla or quiche. Fry them with leftover potatoes or stir into a sauce to go with pasta. Stir them into a creamy sauce, top with breadcrumbs, a savoury crumble topping or grated cheese; and then grill (broil) to make a tempting gratin.

Dry plain cake and stale bread Use dry cake as the base for a trifle, or turn into cake crumbs in a food processor and freeze for later use in crumbles or dessert bakes. Dry bread can be used in bread and butter pudding or made into breadcrumbs for stuffings, gratin toppings or crispy coatings. Alternatively, cut bread into small cubes, fry until crisp and golden and sprinkle over salads or soups for a tasty garnish.

Weights and measures

Keep this conversion guide handy for weights and measures. Use kitchen scales or use cup and spoon measures for dry and solid ingredients and a measuring jug (cup) for liquid ingredients.

Sometimes conversions within a recipe are not exact but are the closest conversion that is a suitable measurement for each system. Use either the metric or the imperial measurements; do not mix the two systems.

🍃 1 metric cup equals 250 ml. Imperial cup measures are smaller than the metric sizes, i.e. 1 cup is 8 fl oz (235 ml).

🍃 A small variation in the weight or volume of most ingredients is unlikely to adversely affect a recipe. The exceptions are yeast, baking powder and bicarbonate of soda (baking soda); for these ingredients, adjust the quantity accordingly.

🍃 In Australia a standard tablespoon is 20 ml, whilst British, New Zealand, North American and South African tablespoons are 15 ml (½ fl oz).

🍃 If a recipe uses 20 ml tablespoons and you have a 15 ml (½ fl oz) tablespoon, add an extra teaspoon for each tablespoon specified.

Weight conversions

10 g	¼ oz	315 g	10 oz
15 g	½ oz	345 g	11 oz
30 g	1 oz	375 g	12 oz (¾ lb)
60 g	2 oz	410 g	13 oz
90 g	3 oz	440 g	14 oz
125 g	4 oz (¼ lb)	470 g	15 oz
155 g	5 oz	500 g	16 oz (1 lb)
185 g	6 oz	750 g	24 oz (1½ lb)
220 g	7 oz	1 kg	32 oz (2 lb)
250 g	8 oz (½ lb)	1.5 kg	48 oz (3 lb)
280 g	9 oz	2 kg	64 oz (4 lb)

Pan sizes and capacity

20 cm	8 inch	mini muffin pan:		
23 cm	9 inch	30 ml	2 tablespoons	
25 cm	10 inch	regular muffin pan:		
2 litre	2 quart	80 ml	⅓ cup	

Metric cup and spoon sizes

¼ cup	60 ml	¼ teaspoon	1.25 ml
⅓ cup	80 ml	½ teaspoon	2.5 ml
½ cup	125 ml	1 teaspoon	5 ml
1 cup	250 ml	2 teaspoons	10 ml
2 cups	500 ml	1 tablespoon	20 ml

Cup conversions

Many recipes will give the weight and volume as well as the cup amount, but keep this list handy for some common ingredients and their weight for 1 metric cup.

Dry ingredients (weight by metric cup)

breadcrumbs, dry	100 g	3 ½ oz
butter, soft	250 g	8 oz
cheese, grated	125 g	4 oz
coconut, desiccated	90 g	3 ¼ oz
flour	150 g	5 oz
mixed fruit, dried	185 g	6 oz
rice, uncooked	200 g	7 oz
sour cream	250 g	8 oz
sugar, brown – lightly packed	185 g	6 oz
sugar, brown – firmly packed	220 g	7 oz
sugar, caster/superfine	220 g	7 oz
sugar, icing/confectioners'	125 g	4 oz
sugar, white	220 g	7 oz
yogurt	250 g	8 oz

Liquid ingredients (volume by metric cup)

¼ cup	60 ml	2 fl oz
⅓ cup	80 ml	2 ½ fl oz
½ cup	125 ml	4 fl oz
¾ cup	180 ml	6 fl oz
1 cup	250 ml	8 ¾ fl oz
1 ¼ cups	310 ml	10 ½ fl oz
1 ½ cups	375 ml	13 fl oz
1 ¾ cups	430 ml	15 fl oz
2 cups	500 ml	17 fl oz
2 ½ cups	625 ml	21 ½ fl oz
3 cups	750 ml	26 fl oz
4 cups	1 L	35 fl oz
5 cups	1.25 L	44 fl oz
6 cups	1.5 L	52 fl oz
8 cups	2 L	70 fl oz
10 cups	2.5 L	88 fl oz

My Favourite Recipes

Text and compilation Deborah Nixon
Text (Kitchen Notes) Janine Flew
Copy Editor Katri Hilden
Designer Melanie Young
Photography cover/chapter openers Andre Martin
Stylist Gabrielle Wheatley
Proofreader Susan McCreery
Senior Production Controller Monique Tesoriero
Production Manager – Books Susan Maffucci

Reader's Digest General Books

Editorial Director Elaine Russell
Managing Editor Rosemary McDonald
Art Director Carole Orbell

My Favourite Recipes is published by
Reader's Digest (Australia) Pty Limited
80 Bay Street, Ultimo NSW 2007
www.readersdigest.com.au,
www.readersdigest.co.nz,
www.readersdigest.co.za

First published 2009
Copyright © Reader's Digest (Australia) Pty Limited 2009
Copyright © Reader's Digest Association Far East
Limited 2009 Philippines
Copyright © Reader's Digest Association Far East
Limited 2009

ISBN 978-1-921569-40-1

®Reader's Digest and The Digest logo are registered
trademarks of The Reader's Digest Association, Inc., of
Pleasantville, New York, USA.

Prepress by Sinnott Bros, Sydney
Printed and bound by Leo Paper Products, China

We are interested in receiving your comments on the
contents of this book. Write to: The Editor, General Books
Editorial, Reader's Digest (Australia) Pty Limited,
GPO Box 4353, Sydney, NSW 2001,
or email us at bookeditors.au@readersdigest.com

Photography

p7 iStock; p7 (wooden spoons) Photodisc; p169 iStock;
p170 iStock. Images not listed are copyright © Reader's Digest.

Recipes

All recipes are copyright © Reader's Digest.
For more recipes, see *The Complete Book of Herbs,
Midweek Meals made Easy, Healthy One-Dish Cooking,
Vegetables for Vitality, The Great Potato Cookbook,
Super Salads* and *Baking with Love* from Reader's Digest.

With thanks to The Essential Ingredient.

Product code 041 3961